WOR TOMIS THE POLIS

(OUR THOMAS THE POLICEMAN)

TOM CURRY

Published by Tom Curry Email: tomwcurry@gmail.com

Printed by Book Printing UK www.bookprintinguk.com

Remus House, Coltsfoot Drive, Peterborough, PE2 9BF

Printed in Great Britain

ISBN 978-1-80049-096-3

'I can't remember being attached to the Special Branch.'

BEST WISHES TOM CURRY

DEDICATION

Dedicated to my Dad, Mam, and the Curry Family

ACKNOWLEDGEMENTS

Amble In Old Photographs. Bartle Rippon.

Linda Ridgewell and Family. Ronnie Johnson and Family.

The Morton Family. Jon Anthoni Cooper.

The unknown originators of some photographs.

Rosie Walton at Book Printing UK.

<u>NOTE</u>. I am aware that this book is no literary masterpiece but I do hope it is both fun and informative. It has been 100% produced, during the unprecedented UK 'lockdown' situation, by an ordinary guy, without a proofreader, editor, publisher or any other assistance in this field, except for the straightforward printing, to my specifications.

This less common way to produce a book is the only way I could recover my costs. I refuse to allow my work to enhance the income of those, with a lesser input than myself or to incur their exorbitant fees. I've never been afraid of criticism, to be different or to 'have a go.' If I have failed to spot and correct any minor print errors, I do apologise but I trust that it will not detract from the reader's enjoyment and the all-important content.

FOREWORD

WARNING........My humour has helped me combat adversity and without it, my life would not have been half as enjoyable. I can see the funny side of most things. The same as if we were to meet, if I think of something that might be amusing at whatever moment, I will share it with you, for I fear not to would inhibit me. I want to enjoy the writing of this book as much as I would hope any reader might.

In parts, I will try to lighten the mood by letting my vivid imagination run free without straying from the truth. I will endeavour to tell the tale at times, in a stand-up comedic style and as if I am just talking to you. After all, laughter they say is the best form of medicine. Mind you, I have found that depending on what it is you are suffering from, antibiotics will take some beating!

In some pieces when referring to my time in Northumberland and any direct speech quoted from a Geordie speaker it might be fun to write/spell it as it would sound. (Soond.)

There are many serious moments to come but without my humour, I would cease to be Tom Curry.

CONTENTS   PAGES

CHAPTER 1

AMBLE, THE CURRY AND PURVIS FAMILY

Thomas William Curry, later to be known simply as Tom or 'Wor Tomis The Polis,' (Wor is our and Polis is the police, in the NE Geordie dialect) was born on 14 October 1949, to parents Fred and Emma Curry, at 26, Newburgh Street, Amble Northumberland.

Amble is a small NE coastal town with a population back then of just under 5000. The main available work was coal mining or fishing but the fishing was mainly confined to a small group of families. Railway tracks crisscrossed through the middle of the town, allowing steam trains to deliver wagons of coal to be loaded onto ships at the bustling harbour, which included the thriving fishing fleet.

In the worst winter weather, scores of Dutch herring boats would seek refuge in the harbour to avoid the fiercest gales, tying up alongside, perhaps 3 or 4 abreast. As a child, how odd I thought it was to hear men talking in a tongue I could not understand, whilst they clomped about in wooden shoes. Often the savage NE gales were not predicted and the men who crewed the fleet found themselves stranded for days and without UK currency. They would set up barrels on the decks and smoke some of their catch of herrings. The resulting kippers were then sold to locals, in return for cash urgently required for beer money and other ashore items. The locals welcomed them and there were few if any problems experienced.

I was the youngest by 7 years of 5 children. In order of age, they were Elizabeth (Betty) Alan, Raymond, Kathleen and then me.

My Dad had been born on St. Valentine's Day in 1907. His parents were farmworkers and he had 3 brothers and 1 sister. His elder brother Andrew Curry, Private 15913, Northumberland Fusiliers, died of wounds at The Somme in WW1. He was 21 years and 9 months old.

My mother was a couple of years younger than my Dad. Her parents were farmworkers too and she was one of 7 children. Her father had been killed after falling from a horse and cart, leaving his widow with the unenviable task of bringing up the 7 young children on her own. She never remarried and was a resilient and tough woman. She did a good job and none of the 7 ever gave her cause for concern.

My sister Betty, who was 14 years older than me, lived with her first husband in Amble They had 2 children together, Gordon and Julie. Gordon is, of course, my nephew but I am only 13 years older than him. Betty worked locally for the Co-op delivering milk with a motorised pedestrian milk float, including down our street and I would help her on occasions. To deliver to houses at the Salt Pans, instead of trying to negotiate an unmade road, she would leave the float unattended in Links Road and walk. Nothing was ever missing when she returned.

My brother Alan was 13 years older than me and desperately wanted to join the RAF but was refused entry as a prospective pilot because he wore glasses. He was offered ground crew but he said he could not bear to be around planes if he could not fly them. So instead, he joined the army, the R.E.M.E. This was thought at the time, to be an act of revenge. He did pursue his lifelong obsession for flying in his spare time and you will hear more of that later.

Whilst in the army he met Cyril Moyle, from Worthing in Sussex, who was also in Alan's regiment. They became great friends and sometimes Cyril would spend his leave with Alan and us in Amble. Other times Alan would visit Worthing with Cyril. Ironically, Cyril met his future wife, Audrey Shanks, in Amble and after leaving the army he moved there, where he spent the rest of his life. He became well known and was a popular manager at The Radcliffe social club in Amble, until his retirement. Alan did the opposite of Cyril and he met his wife in Worthing. On leaving the army he settled there, working for Birds Eye frozen foods. . Without lovely Cyril, none of us 3 Curry sons would have moved south to Sussex

In his early 20s, Ray also moved south in search of work and for a while, he too lived Worthing, in lodgings. He met his future wife in Brighton and settled there for a period. They had 2 sons, Rory and Jamie. Ray trained as a carpenter and two big jobs he worked on were Brighton Marina and the Thames Barrier. Ray's ex-landlord, when he first moved to Worthing, Matt Wilson, was a fine man and I got to know him very well, which you will read about later.

My sister Kath, who was 7 years older than me, moved away to take up live-in domestic work. Many years later, after being a bus conductress, she passed her test and became a driver for the United Bus Company. She was only the second female within the company to do so and I was impressed. She had never driven anything before and had passed her test the first time and on a double-decker bus. She later married and had one son, Alan.

As the youngest, I can only remember Ray and Kath living at home. Ray and I are the sole survivors of the 5 children. So having described the Curry's and the extended family, I will begin the story of the events that unfolded.

A rarity for the Curry's to be all together.

Alan   Raymond/Ray

Elizabeth/Betty   Kathleen/Kath   Mam   Dad

Thomas/Tom

CHAPTER 2

THE WAR YEARS

When WW2 broke out my father was working on a farm and as such he was exempt from being conscripted. He was married and had 2 children by then but he waived his right of exemption and willingly volunteered his services. He was inducted into the Royal Engineers, becoming Sapper 1914417, John Frederick Curry.

All my life I considered my Uncle Andrew a war hero. I researched his history and this strengthened my belief. I vowed that if I ever had a son, I would call him Andrew but I never did father a child. I researched my Dad's service record and I realised that I had missed recognising another real hero, my Dad. I say this because Andrew volunteered for something, not knowing exactly what terrible fate awaited him and thousands of others.

My Dad had seen his brother killed in WW1 and being exempt still went ahead and volunteered for WW2. From his service record, I found him to have been, 5' 6½'' tall weighing only 138lbs and with a 37-inch chest. Why would such a quiet and reserved man of quite a small stature, volunteer for war service knowing he could face death as his brother had? I cannot with any certainty say I would do what he did, with the death of my brother preying on my mind.

Royal Engineers Sapper 1914417 John Frederick Curry.

By the time I had realised my mistake both my Mam and Dad had died but I put the question to my eldest sister Betty, as to what drove our Dad to volunteer for WW2. She simply replied, "Dad saw many others go, including our Uncle Tom (my namesake and Mam's brother) and Dad said that he had to play his part too." I believe he was a true hero to do that.

Dad served in North Africa, Italy and France and on discharge his military conduct was described as 'Very Good.'

Whilst serving in Italy, as the war raged, a very unlikely occurrence took place. Uncle Tom my Mam's brother had joined up around the same time and was in the Northumberland Fusiliers. Tom and

Fred had left Amble not knowing where either might be sent. They said their goodbye's and wished each other good luck and hoped they would be reunited on their safe return. Neither knew where their initial posting was to be let alone the other's ultimate destination. Fred was first sent to North Africa and then moved on to Italy. It was in Italy that he developed an abscess on his cheek. The medication of the day at first failed to work and due to the heat, he became quite unwell and was admitted to hospital. As he perhaps forlornly lay in bed thinking of his family back home, Uncle Tom walked through the ward. He had got a piece of shrapnel in his arm.

The unlikely early reunion in such a far off country and during the war must have brought them such unbelievable joy. The two soldiers had little chance of meeting and it was all the more remarkable in that they were from entirely separate regiments. If they had been in the same country and area, how odd that they both needed hospital treatment and found themselves at the same hospital, let alone the same ward. When Tom had gone to the hospital, he may not have had cause to visit the very ward in which Fred was housed and they may have missed each other by a matter of a few feet. I am still astounded now by the amazing coincidence and so how they must felt is beyond me. What a joyous day that must have been for the soldier pair.

WOR GLADYS DECLARES WAR ON THE NATIONAL COAL BOARD

The next story is true but I have written it in what I hope is a humorous and entertaining way;

My Uncle, Tom Purvis, his wife Gladys and their two daughters, Sylvia and Joyce, lived in Henderson Street, Amble, only a few streets away from us. As the coal mines began to close in Northumberland in the late 50s early 60s, Tom with his family moved to Yorkshire, where the coal mining industry was still booming.

The railway track behind St. Cuthbert's Ave.1960s.

Wor Gladys came to the fore at the outbreak of WW2 with her solo nightly missions.

Gladys was a very active Amble resistance fighter (one-woman band) throughout the war years. In simple terms, she was a successful and prolific NCB coal thief and ruled over her territory, specifically the railway line behind her mother-in-law's home in St. Cuthbert's Ave. Nobody among the menfolk, who were not away at war, dared such an undertaking and so up stepped Gladys, who was the only one who had the bottle it took. It is important to remember that she was not a young woman she was married and had two kids.

Gladys decided she had to do her bit for the war effort and formed her own, mainly solo, nighttime resistance group. She concentrated not on sabotage as such but mainly on 'keeping the home fires burning.' Gladys felt that the wartime slogan gave her the licence to snaffle as much coal as she could get her hands on. She was not intent on 'keeping all the home fires burning' you understand but to be precise, only those of the Purvis clan and close friends, which eventually became most of Henderson St., especially when word spread of her nighttime talent and the rewards it provided.

Rumour had it, that when Hauxley colliery announced they were struggling to keep up with the war demands, Gladys momentarily considered offering to sell her stock back to them, just to be seen as helping out. Gladys looked elderly even when she was young and had the build of a starving whippet, weighing in at less than 6 stone and was 5' nothing in height but apparently, she had the extraordinary ability to carry a sack of coal at least 50% heavier than her body weight. It is safe to say that from her appearance no one would suspect what her nighttime occupation was, including the local cops.

Gladys said she, like her husband Tom, had her pit togs (work clothes) for when she was on the night shift. She persuaded/ forced my eldest brother Alan who was about 8 at the time to go on a night raid with her, mainly just to act as a lookout. Most nights Gladys courageously operated alone. Perhaps, with blackened faces, the unlikely duo ventured forth soon after nightfall. My brother then was built like a stick and was so young he couldn't compete with his Auntie Gladys when it came to any weight-lifting competition. So on the railway line behind St. Cuthbert's Ave. the most frequent of crime scenes of this nature the partners in crime put their daring plan into operation.

Gladys first checked the wagon tickets to see what load they were carrying. This expert didn't want any old rubbish, just the sought after best coal nuggets would do for her. Alan was told to stay on the ground and fill the sack with what she threw down after she had scaled the wagon. He was instructed to let her know when the sack was full or if he saw anyone approaching.

Up Gladys went on to the top of the wagon and began throwing down to Alan the best big lumps. After a while, she must have thought that has to be enough and called to Alan as loud as she dared. No reply and so down she went to find poor little Alan spark-out having been hit on the head. She managed to bring him around enough to set off for home. Gladys' route was less direct but unlike others, chose not to take the shortest more risky street route. Oh! No, Gladys was much too wily for that, she'd cut through the allotments and then back on to the railway track leading home to the rear of Henderson St. However, on this occasion en-route and in the dark Gladys encountered a large hole half-filled with water. Gladys with sack fell headfirst and completely submerged disappearing into the murky water.

According to my brother, his Auntie Gladys instantly emerged spluttering but still with the coal sack on her back. She was not going to let go of the valuable booty. She must have looked as if she were some sort of soaked, khaki-clad saboteur. (wet/mud from head to toe.) It was rumoured that Gladys had during the war years transported and recycled more coal than Hauxley pit and the NCB put together. The others were in a completely different lower league to Wor Gladys, more like apprentices in comparison. By the way, you cannot blame him but my brother Alan never went on another night raid. That was him done, his first and last. I still to this day just cannot understand why my Auntie Gladys was never awarded a George Cross for her valiant war efforts in 'keeping the home fires burning.' (at least for the Purvis', Henderson St. and an ever-increasing group of friends.) A posthumous award might be still possible with your support.

Unfortunately, there is a sad ending, as coal came to its end Wor Gladys seemed to lose interest in life and lived quietly but comfortably in a gas centrally heated home in Yorkshire. After failing to become Gorgi registered, she was never the same after the coming of gas and just could not adapt to it in the same way as she had 'managed' the era of coal. She gave up and finally retired to a peaceful but uneventful and unexciting life. Gladys was always years ahead of her time and not waiting like us, until the outbreak of the Covid-19 pandemic, she was a true pioneer and took to wearing a mask at the start of the war in 1939. Spare a thought the next time you see a photo-fit on Crimewatch because it just might be, Wor Gladys!

NOTE. Daughters, Sylvia and Joyce also carried on a similar occupation to their Mam but I cannot reveal the true nature but what I can say is, it does also involve night work and sacks!

Wor Gladys, I am sure you will agree was a true character and a one-off.

After the war, Fred returned to the UK to his wife and family but with no job waiting for him. After a period of unemployment, he was forced to take the only work available, coal mining. During his unemployment, struggling to provide for his family and with rationing still in place, he was to make a decision that would have a profound effect on him.

Uncle Tom had also left the forces and was back living in Amble with his wife, Gladys and their 2 daughters. He too was without work and struggling to support his family. Tom hatched a plan that one night he would raid a farmer's field for some potatoes. He persuaded Fred to accompany him and so as night fell off they went. Tom quickly filled his small bag and said he would go on ahead to a turnip patch to get a single turnip. On his way to fetch a turnip, Fred was apprehended by a policeman and taken off to the police station.

Tom escaped capture but Fred subsequently appeared before a court and was fined a few shillings. My Dad broke his heart and was devastated. What he repeated many times during his life, was how he had gotten to the age of nearly forty and had gone all through the war with an unblemished record and then for that to happen. As I see it, drastic times called for drastic action. After all, can you condemn a man for a few potatoes and a turnip after returning from war to find his job had gone and he is forced to live on meagre handouts? Yes, it was wrong but Fred was a decent good man and this one-off misdemeanour haunted him for the rest of his life. That was punishment enough irrespective of the few shillings he was fined.

CHAPTER 3

GROWING UP IN AMBLE

My Dad began his new life as a Northumbrian coal miner. He was a reserved quiet man and appeared to be well-liked by all. He was a conscientious and good worker.

After my home birth, we continued to live in the terraced house at 26, Newburgh St. and Dad was then working at Hauxley Colliery (referred to in the NE as, 'doon the pit') The house was owned by the pit, as were all the others in our street but we only occupied the first floor, consisting of a living room with black range coal fire and 2 separate bedrooms. There was no bathroom or toilet. There was only a single cold water tap in the backyard shared with the flat downstairs, as was the dry toilet referred to in the NE as the 'ootside netty.' The netty could not be more primitive or unappealing, being only a wooden seat over a hole in the ground. There was no plumbing or heating or lighting. Toilet paper was an old newspaper cut into squares and threaded onto a string that hung on a nail on the wall. If my Dad had not read the paper he would hold a mirror to my bottom and then he was able to read it from the ink imprint in the reflection of the mirror! The ashes from the coal fire were sprinkled inside the toilet hole but that was the only control substance ever added.

I know from visiting friends who remained in Newburgh Street that it was the only toilet facility right up into the 60's and two families continued to share it. Adjacent to the toilet was a coal house and also in the yard was a wash-house with cast-iron pot for boiling clothes being heated from underneath from a grated coal fire. Bathing took place by the fire in the living room in a tin bath. Water was either heated on the range or in the washhouse. Either way, it meant water at some stage was carried upstairs be it in a hot state or cold whatever the preference was but it also necessarily involved the bailing out of the bath too. Suffice it to say it was a major event involving a considerable amount of work just to have a bath, which we all now take for granted and with such ease and minimum effort. It was heavy work carried out mainly by the womenfolk and some families had 2 or 3 pitmen in the home, so the workload was multiplied.

The rear of Newburgh Street.

In the 1980s on one of my visits back to Amble, I went to the rear of Newburgh St. and I took a photograph to show the last remaining lowest wooden door to access the dry toilet. All the others had been bricked up. The midden men we called them, were employed by the council. They opened the access door and used a shovel to clear the contents loading it onto a lorry. This undesirable task was still taking place well into the 60s. The other higher doors are to allow easy access to empty sacks of coal into the coal house area.

Now kids have computers but back then we amused ourselves in more simple ways. You haven't lived until you have made your own fun by noisily opening the netty access door and then to see the startled occupant scuttle across the backyard to return indoors, whilst still adjusting their dress on the way, thinking 'the midden men aren't due today.' If you were one of those victims, I now feel suitably cleansed, as I ask for forgiveness! I wouldn't do much for the Amble tourist trade, would I? Who needs coastal views IF I am to be your guide but it is part of the town's history. I bet you will look closer, next time you are there.

Bath time for the pitman.

This is obviously a posed photograph but I've kept it for many years because it is as near as you might get to what went on, up into the 60s in Newburgh St., (and across the UK) every day when the men returned home from the pit. Our room looked exactly like that.

These poorly paid, brave guys worked in danger of gas, flooding and cave-in, with only a naked flame carbide lamp to show the way. They relied on canaries to keep them safe from gassing and worked alongside pit ponies. I remember seeing my Dad fill a Tizer bottle with water every time he left for work and place it in his bait bag. (Bait, is a Geordie word for lunch.) The most frequently carried bags were the canvas recycled WW2 gas mask bags. When he returned home he emptied the bottle and refilled it before he left again. He never told me why he carried out this daily ritual but never did he drink any of the water, in all his working days. I knew that water and tea were available down below but it only dawned on me after my Dad died, that the only reason he did it was that he feared a cave in and being trapped. What a way to earn a living, eh?

Links Road thronged with armies of weary coal dust-covered men, in their filthy pit work clothes, as they trudged home from Hauxley colliery, at all hours of the day and night after a shift of hard graft.

My Mam made all the decisions, frequently the wrong ones but my Dad was so easygoing he just soaked it all up without complaint. My Mam showered Betty and Kath with affection but Dad was all for the boys. I spent more time with Dad than Mam and it was always Dad who saw me off to school. It is correct to

17

say that theirs was not a happy marriage and on one occasion, although I cannot remember it, my Dad left and lived for a short period with his sister, Anne. He returned shortly after but nothing much changed. During this time I was the only sibling left at home. My parents slept in separate rooms and there were periods when they did not communicate and the atmosphere could be frosty. I never went short of love but it was more so from Dad.

A MOVE TO LINKS AVE. WITH ALL 'MOD CONS'

We moved to a new council house at 47, Links Ave. in about 1955. For the first time, we had an inside toilet and initially, my parents thought it might not be hygienic! It took over 30 minutes to walk to Hauxley colliery. From our kitchen window and upstairs rear window, we could see across a caravan site and fields to Hauxley pit heap, 2 ½ miles away.

View from rear of 47, Links Ave. of Hauxley colliery pit heap in the distance. It was closed then and the cage wheel and buildings had been removed, as was the heap much later.

Cyril Moyle, (Alan's R.E.M.E. friend) Alan, Raymond and me
at the front door of 47, Links Ave.

Opposite our home lived a lovely childless couple, Ted and Bet
Stanley. Ted had lost an arm and had a false one. The hand was
covered by a brown leather glove. The couple at Christmas used to
store neighbours presents for the kids in their home. Just after
midnight Christmas Day, Ted would dress as Santa and deliver to
the Links Avenue kids. Sadly his one gloved false hand never
fooled me.

On one of Santa's visits, my Dad gave him a Woodbine cigarette as he left us. Ted's face had a dressing on it on Christmas Day. Santa had set his beard alight. He'd been patched up, a new beard quickly found and Santa had bravely carried on with his home visits. It must have helped Santa bear the pain, that he'd had a refreshment drink in every house, although the drink may have contributed to the accident in the first place. You could not make it up, could you? A one-armed Geordie speaking, tipsy, Woodbine smoking, Santa with his beard on fire!

OUR PET DOG BOXER

Whilst living at 47, Links Ave, we acquired a pet dog, a black labrador/collie crossbreed and we named him Boxer. He was a placid beast and we had him for about 13 years. However, he was involved in an accident with Tait's ice cream van in our street. It was not the lovely Jacky Tait's fault but he was deeply saddened. The poor pet went right underneath the van and was in a bad way and we were all upset. The vet told us that the most humane thing to do was to have him put to sleep because he had sustained serious back injuries and would never be able to walk again.

My Mam refused to have him put to sleep and said that we'd keep him a week or two to see if he improved. Boxer eventually started to drag himself about with his front legs. The vet was consulted again and he said there was now the slimmest chance that he might regain some movement but he would never be the same.

My Mam dedicated herself to do everything to try and get him back to as he was but initially it looked like a hopeless case. Day

20

after day she exercised Boxer by rolling up a towel, putting it under his belly next to his back legs and then walking him forward whilst supporting his weight with the towel. Gradually over many months, Boxer improved and eventually a miracle happened and he fully recovered.

I do not think for one minute the miracle was performed by God, it was my Mam with a rolled towel that healed Boxer.

Boxer and our pet cat, Kitty, albeit a male, were firm friends. Kitty is the cat with me in the photograph taken at the rear of Newburgh St. on the front cover. Although placid with me, as can be seen, he was a fighter and lost an eye later on in his life. He then gained the second name of Nelson.

AMBLE INFANTS SCHOOL

I began my schooldays at Amble infants and it was there, for the first time, I made a class laugh. I was put into school early at age 4. One day the female teacher, the lovely Mrs Gair, met my Mam at the school gates and said, "Your Thomas has had the staff in fits of laughter today when I told them of what took place. I was trying to teach his class the time and they were not quite getting it. I said, it's easy and raising my voice slightly and pointing to the clock chalked on the board, I said, it's, 1 o'clock, 2 o'clock, 3 o'clock. Before I got the next words out, Thomas shouted out, ROCK!" She said she had to compose herself to carry on and had told the other teachers at break time.

It must have been even funnier coming from such a young and tiny kid, I guess. Mam related the story repeatedly over the years. I reckon that was the very beginning of my humour and my desire to amuse and bring about the beautiful sound of laughter and the satisfaction I have always gained by being able to switch it on. Google reveals it was in 1954 that Bill Hayley and 'Rock around the clock' hit the charts, which was the inspiration for my outburst.

My first clear memory of my childhood is of being at the hall in Dovecote St. Amble and a big party on Coronation Day 1953. I guess why I remember it, was the bunting outside but more likely the food, inc. jelly and ice cream etc., the only time I would have seen food like that and in such quantity. Rationing was still on then (until the end of 1954) and I think I can remember seeing a Ration Book with my name on it but later it disappeared.

Kathleen and me.

The photograph was taken in the early 1950s and shows my big sister Kathleen and me. I'm wearing an Indian headdress. My Dad was so sick of me wanting to make one he chased a cockerel and caught it to pull the tail feathers out. Note my sister's hand-knitted cardigan. She looks like the pearly queen of Amble

All our mothers knitted back then, mine being no exception. She knitted everything even my bathers. She seemed oblivious (Maybe she had to, as there was no other choice) to what happened when you went into the water. I have memories of coming out of the sea on the little shore at Amble and the wool was so heavy, the crotch was drooped down by my ankles and I struggled to hold them up. The other kids thought the tide had suddenly gone out or a tsunami was about to hit but it was all in my bathers. I'd emptied the little shore.

Needless to say, I never stood a chance of winning an Olympic medal for swimming. Well not unless they changed the rules so that everyone had to wear knitted bathers! It might be a lot more entertaining, eh?

We need to organise an annual festival on the little shore at Amble and just show the young 'uns how it is done with some panache. So get knitting. Never mind the wet suits they wear at the harbour now, knit them some!

AMBLE FC

My Dad only had one great interest outside the family and that was football. He was a lifelong fan and supporter of the local team, Amble FC. He would attend the home games when he had the entrance fee, which could have only been a few coppers. I cannot remember when he started taking me but it would be either the late 50s or early 60s.

Dad and me.

I remember watching local lad Bobby Lightfoot play for Amble FC. He was strong, powerfully built and fast, a great combination. What a tough good player he was. How I remember spectating in all weathers, no stand, no cover but it still did not deter us on a Saturday and especially as Bobby seemed to score regularly. He was the type of player who would have perfectly fitted into the West Auckland team that won the first 'world cup'. He was bloody hard. I reckon even the so-called tough guy Vinny Jones, would have been easily subdued but Bobby was never a dirty player. We only knew him on the field but he was a pitman. Not only was Bobby my childhood hero and I wished I could play like him but I wanted to be him because my Dad admired his style of play.

NOTE. In 1909, West Auckland Football Club of the Northern League was invited to compete for the prestigious Sir Thomas Lipton trophy in Turin, considered by many to be a precursor to today's World Cup. They went on to win the tournament. Two years later they won it again, thrashing Italian giants Juventus 6-1 in the final.

The film 'A Captain's Tale,' starring Dennis Waterman and Tim Healey, charts the events and is a great watch.

As I say, my Dad was a great supporter of Amble FC, especially of Bobby Lightfoot and I believe he knew a good player when he saw one. Dad had played for a village team, Tritlington FC (1920/30s maybe), along with his 2 brothers, Ed and Jim Curry. How fabulous for 3 brothers to have played alongside one another as adults. I recall there was a photo showing all 3 in their strip posing with the team but sadly it has disappeared. How I wish I could get a duplicate copy and any suggestions would be warmly welcomed?

I am sure any relatives of Bobby will be thrilled to read that he is still remembered.

DAD'S HEALTH FAILS AND THE POVERTY YEARS

About 1955, the pit work took a toll on my poor Dad's health and he was far too frequently off work due to sickness. He suffered from heart trouble and what was described as slight strokes. He would be for example off sick, return to work for a few weeks and be off again, return and then for the same pattern to be repeated over and over again. If you were off sick from the pit after a very short while the pit did not pay you and you had to claim social security. In my youth, we were on that more than not.

As a pit worker, you were given an allowance of free coal and a sectioned tipper lorry would tip a 'load' of coal outside each worker's home. Almost every home in the street would have a pitman in residence and therefore would qualify for the appropriate allowance. The street would be awash with the separate piles of coal on delivery day and at once an army of residents would appear with barrows, buckets, recycled prams and all manner of containers. Within no time the coal was cleared, only leaving remnants of coal dust where the piles had been. Many coal houses were bursting at the seams with stock and some would often be stored outside in the rear garden, covered by tarpaulins or similar material.

There was a very strict rule concerning the allowance and that was that under no circumstances were any of the allowances to be sold, loaned or given away to anyone. It was to be used solely by the residents of and at the allocated home. Any breach of this rule was deemed to be a dismissal offence from the colliery.

26

This brings me to a point where I wish to relate a sorry tale that even now still fills me with sadness. As I have said my Dad was sick more times than he was fit and because of this after a relatively short time his free coal allowance stopped. Therefore, our coal house was almost permanently bare. There was no central heating, no double glazing and the only source of heating and cooking was the open coal fire. You might not only wake up to find ice on the inside of the windows but that water inside the kettle had frequently frozen overnight too. We lived right on the NE coast, only a few hundred yards from the beach, across which a biting winter north wind can blow so harsh that you felt that you would be cut in two.

It distresses me even now to disclose the fact that both my poor parents but especially my dear sick Dad, were forced on to the open Amble beach to scavenge for the lesser quality sea coal that was so hard to find and gather. They were wrapped up in scarves and any warm clothes which might offer the best protection against the atrocious biting weather conditions. How they must have suffered, with me a small child in tow. How shameful that those with burning coals stacked practically up the chimney, with a full coal house, a stash outside too and who could not fail to see us (and others too) struggling from the direction of the beach bearing hard-fought-for scraps of coal, whilst enduring such hardship and did nothing to help.

My dad and our family were not unpopular in the town but not one single person, other than Uncle Joe, ever offered us a bucket of their plentiful coal, not even under the cover of darkness or at

Christmas time too. Our (as others) plight was not unknown as everyone knew each other and most of the time each other's business too. After all, the town's population then was under 5000. The next time you hear propaganda acclaiming the hospitality of the northerners outstripping that of the southerners, try and remember reading these paragraphs. As one who originates from the north but has lived in the south for 50+ years, I can tell you that in my experience no area of the UK is better than the other in this regard and the propaganda has no credibility whatsoever.

My childhood was somewhat underprivileged and I never had what other kids took for granted, for example, I never did have a train set. The only major item I did have was a new bike once but I recall the HP payments were never paid in full. Dad would have been at work when the HP was taken out but I guess soon after he was off sick yet again. Mam organised such stuff and Dad was not consulted, nor did he appear to want to be. Mam was not reckless in such HP matters but because of my Dad's intermittent work pattern, the agreement never seemed to be fulfilled. I remember Mam received numerous threatening letters and court correspondence regarding non-payments. She ended many of her replying letters having explained the situation by adding, 'That's how it is and you cannot get blood out of a stone.' I recall offers of a shilling a week being made but it always seemed that eventually the problem just went away and that was most probably because as we had nothing the ones owed realised it was pointless pursuing matters and just gave up. It was not entirely my parents' fault. My Dad was plagued with ill health, not helped by the pit environment.

Spike Milligan told how he dealt with such debt demands. He said that he wrote back saying that he only had so much money coming in and could not pay everyone. So what he did each month was, he put all the names in a hat of those he had to pay. The first two drawn-out, he paid but if they sent anymore demands he would not even put their names in the hat!

Our home was shabbily furnished mainly from stuff that had seen better days or had been given to us. Both my parents had been on the farms and were the offspring of farmworkers and they are not known for being particularly house proud. My Mam was not good at housekeeping or in money matters, even when Dad was working. At that time many families had a front room that was hardly ever used and so it looked like a showpiece and indeed that is how it was looked upon. We did not have that and the whole house was in disarray. You could look for a pair of scissors or a pen and never find them. The home was not dirty to such an extent that you'd want to exit as fast as you could but it was untidy.

I recall as a kid having an army greatcoat on my bed for many years. It was between the candlewick bedspread and a blanket. I have learnt since that many had the same. Seemingly, this was a make-do, leftover from the war years. It certainly was a good substitute extra blanket. It was effective because they were heavy and known for their warmth. I got so used to it that I was surprised when duvets arrived and I saw they had no sleeves or pockets!

Many years later, I would tease my Mam by relating the story to friends and I could not resist adding my humour. I would say that I didn't understand why every other week the coat changed, from maybe an army corporal's, to an RAF sergeant's or an able seaman's! Poor Mam would say, "Don't say that because people might believe you." It never did stop me.

Early on, I can remember visiting the homes of friends and feeling embarrassed about mine. As far back as I can remember I always took good care of everything I had. When I finally left home what remained behind, was all the books I had ever been given at Christmas etc. They were in mint condition still with the covers. My Mam frequently said that I had been the same with everything right from being a tot. She said that all my toys were kept in a bottom drawer of a chest and if any other kid entered our house, I would sit guard as she put it, next to the drawer.

AMBLE PRIMARY SCHOOL

After infant school, I moved on to primary school which was pretty much uneventful until my last year. In 1961, I was 11 years of age and I was in class 4a being one of about 40. The teacher was a middle-aged man called Mr Donald but all us kids, behind his back, called him Quack. I shall from now on refer to him as Quack because I still cannot bring myself to call him anything other than that, which I think he deserves. It was a particularly unpleasant experience to be in his class, as he clearly did not like me and in my opinion, he should never have been in the teaching profession. Quite simply, I despised him and found him to be little more than an immature bully. He was gentler with the girls especially the brighter of them and maybe that was because he found them of no challenge to his ego.

He only really wanted boffin types in his class and treated the ordinary or slower with almost disinterest, if not contempt. I certainly fell into his contempt category even though I never did consider that I was slow academically. I accept I only ever did sufficient to keep myself above the lower end of the class and around the middle was good enough for me and was easily achievable without any effort. I could have worked harder but I much preferred to have fun and make people laugh than being studious. I was not the 'dimwit' he called me on numerous occasions and he often used the same reference to describe our part of the class. I was the class clown but Quack underestimated me and he must have put no bearing on the saying 'it takes a clever man to be a clown.' He was an advocate of 'empty vessels make the most sound' and referenced that many times, particularly in my case. I suggest where life took me is proof that there is more credence in the former than his biased opinion.

I appreciate as an 11-12-year-old kid that others, if not subjected to his detrimental treatment would not pick up on it as an adult would. On the receiving end, it was far from being acceptable behaviour from a teacher especially to such young and vulnerable pupils. Nearly 60 years on Quack is in the past and unimportant but I was there and still have the lasting memory.

Let me give you an example of his outlandish behaviour which I merely witnessed. It did not concern me, which will hopefully demonstrate my unbiased account of an incident where I was not the target. I will give the poor victim the fictitious name of Michael. He was called to the front of the entire class of 40 by Quack and told to remove his sock and shoe and to hold his foot up so everyone could see.

The class were encouraged to come forward if they could not see. His foot was filthy to the extent it was blackened with engrained dirt. Michael was always a scruffy kid but he was an 11- year-old, so it was not entirely his fault. That poor kid was publicly humiliated in front of the whole class. I would imagine Quack had seen his feet as he changed for PT or such like and had premeditated the reprehensible cruel act. My heart aches for the kid as I recount the sorry tale. I never discussed it nor have I seen Michael since those school days.

As far as I was concerned my special treatment was that I was made to sit at a single desk on my own, not in one of the other 4 lines, which Quack referred to as 'your cage' i.e. 'get back in your cage.' There were 4 lines of desks facing the front of the class, the deemed brightest were to the right in order of test results working down to the lowest in the class on the left. However, irrespective of my results, I was in a special place. My desk was not in a row, it was on its own at the front left of class and instead of facing front, it faced at an angle towards the windows.

I was not a wild kid or unlikeable but I did have a talent for making people laugh, especially those to the left of class where I was situated, He saw this as disruption and being devoid of any humour himself, singled me out for the special treatment. I accept it may have been annoying but it was not constant and other teachers seemed to like me.

He waited until he was acting head and he, deliberately I believe, orchestrated a situation that required my punishment. What he did was, he stood me in front of the whole class and belted me with the official big leather belt on both hands. This was unheard of because it incapacitated your writing hand and surely must have been reserved for the most serious of misdemeanours? Mine was so minor that I cannot remember what it was but I could have easily been targeted for talking in class, maybe.

If you forget my being belted on both hands, to carry out the punishment publicly was absolutely outside the rules. It was by no coincidence that it took place whilst the head, Mr Bowman was absent and Quack was deputising. To my knowledge, no kid had ever been belted on both hands, even for stealing or fighting and never outside the privacy of the head's office. I could not have been so bad because I was no acquaintance of the school belt. Quack's attempt to bully me into submission or make me cry in front of the class didn't work as I was too tough for that. It would have certainly made others in the class sit up and focus.

Another time, Quack said that in his day, if a kid disrupted a class learning they were 'sent to Coventry.' He heavily suggested that should be my treatment. The next thing I knew was most of the class, except for a couple of closest chums, were acting as if I did not exist. A friend told me a list was being compiled and was signed by those who agreed to stop speaking to me and the list was in the organiser's desk. He was in the top boffin group. Acting on the advice of my brother, Ray, I got to his desk at playtime and took possession of the list. I hit the one who had compiled it and told the others on the list I knew they'd signed it and they'd better start speaking to me. As expected it worked and very soon normality was restored.

Quack's specialist subject was art and I was always exceptionally good at that and consistently top of the class and that continued into his class 4a. As proof, I was awarded the book prize that year in 4a for art and craft. As I got older I found I was more crafty than arty! The odd thing was Quack would constantly be around me during art lessons acting like some old buddy. He appeared to switch on a like for me but off it would go again, at the end until the next art lesson. I heard him on a couple of occasions when I had praise from the head say, "I told him it would be better if he," this and that as if he should be rewarded for my natural ability. If some artwork was considered exceptional it would be displayed not in the classroom but instead in the hall with the head making the final decision. My work was frequently exhibited in the hall. Listen to me, Michaelangelo! I'm no shrinking violet, am I? To be honest, it is difficult to be humble, if you are that good, isn't it?!

I was a pretty tough streetwise kid even at that tender age. I was a leader, not a follower but never a bully, perhaps with one exception, a girl in our class who had a crush on me, which I found uncomfortable. Looking back I may have bullied her, not physically but verbally. I rejected her attentions but any abuse could only have been minor as she appeared to get keener. If I bump into her I'll apologise but only if she guarantees me she won't start up again.

It would have been pointless if I had passed the 11+ because we could never have afforded the additional grammar school finance. As it was I never did wear a school uniform, or any small part of it, that was requested but not compulsory, when I moved up to the secondary modern school.

I was 11 ½ when I left primary school and moved on to the secondary modern school. Those who had passed the 11+ then moved to the grammar school in nearby Alnwick, some 10 miles distant. I never again had anything more to do with any of those who had been in 4a with me. We lived in the same small town and could not help but see one another out and about but they mixed together and those of us attending the secondary modern in Amble did the same.

Dr R. P. Robertson

Dr Robertson practised in Amble from 1946 to 1976 and was our family doctor up until we left the area in about 1963. He sometimes had breathing difficulties himself and often was in a worse condition than the patients he attended but he was never known to miss a call, even if he was a little grumpy perhaps because of his well-being on occasions. However, we all respected him and accepted his character, knowing Amble was lucky to have him. He was on call 24/7 and if needed urgently you called at his home/surgery out of hours in Oswald St. To my knowledge no one ever left untreated irrespective of the hour. His work took him down the pit and to sea on the Amble lifeboat. He was a great doctor to have. I believe he had been an officer Dr/Surgeon in WW2.

In Amble then, it took longer to get transport to the hospital and so his skills were a bonus. When I was about 9, I vividly remember an occasion when he saved the day. My brother Ray worked at Hauxley pit.

One day in about 1958, my mother and I were at Ronnie Jones grocery van when Mr Coxford from 53 Links Ave. approached us. He was blackened with coal dust and had come hotfoot straight from the pit. He handed my Mam one wellington (a shock in itself) and said Ray had been hurt at the pit and would be brought home in some sort of improvised transport very soon. Ray had been on bank (the pit surface) and was crossing a track when a run-away tub had smashed into him and severely crushed his inner thigh.

Poor Ray who was about 18/19 was brought into 47 Links Ave. He was semi-conscious and shaking uncontrollably. He was laid out on the floor in front of the open coal fire in the front room. The fire was stoked up and beds were quickly raided and the covers were piled up high on top of Ray. I remember peeping through the gap between the door frame and the door and seeing Dr Robertson set to, cutting large pieces of flesh from the injury as he carried out quite major surgery. The bruised and damaged flesh was put into a bowl and disposed of, on the other open fire in the kitchen.

I considered whether or not to give that last detail but it is true and was the best way of disposal available. I also feel that it also gives a true account of pit village life and how the emergency treatment was dealt with when hospital transport was not so readily available in 1958. The leg was saved, without any after-effects barring a very large scar. Ray and our family were always grateful to Dr Robertson and his skills, especially when he not for the first time saved the day and undoubtedly my big brother's leg, in a make-shift operating theatre, on the floor in front of the fire, in the front room of 47, Links Ave. Amble.

Dr Robertson used asthma inhalers himself. He first prescribed them for me in about 1961. I used them for about 25 years until I stopped using them and now I do not suffer from any asthma problems. He rightly predicted all those years ago that I could eventually grow out of it but it did take longer than anyone anticipated.

It is well reported that his pet hate was Lucozade and every time he spotted it, he would say something like, "Have you got money to throw away on that stuff? Tizer is considerably cheaper and will do the same job."

AMBLE SECONDARY MODERN SCHOOL

The secondary modern school was at what we called the top end of Amble and we lived at the bottom and it was about a mile walk to school every day. The headmaster was a man called Mr Johnstone, his wife was also a teacher at the school and she taught science. The head also taught science and occasionally he took my class for science lessons. He was a big man but there again every adult looked big to me then but in his case he was. I remember his lessons were extremely dull. I learnt early on that he did not appear to have much in the way of a sense of humour and because of this and maybe the fact he was the one who wielded the dreaded cane with much gusto, I avoided taking any witty chances with him.

I remember frequently at the morning assembly, at what seemed any given opportunity, he referenced an ex-head boy. He had been a head-boy when I was at the school and so I knew of him. The head's frequent referencing reason was that he had joined the Northumbria police and was a constable stationed in Amble. The head constantly referred to him as being a role model.

The constable's home posting to Amble, I consider was an unusual decision, believing it to be entirely unnecessary, the factor being the small population of 5000. He had grown up in the town and his antecedents would be known to most. I also believe there is never a perfect kid and this could at times have caused him problems. Familiarity breeds contempt they say and I witnessed an example of this perhaps when I revisited Amble in 1969 when I was 20. I too was a PC living in Sussex at the time and I was with my PC (later Sergeant) friend, Alan Trussler, on a short break.

It was about 11 pm in the main street in Amble. There was a group of youths behaving rowdily and the ex-head boy PC was in attendance together with another colleague. My friend and I viewed the scene with interest. Time and time again, he warned the group regarding their behaviour to no avail and was met with chants of his surname and swearing. I thought the chaotic scene to be an embarrassment to the police and there should have been some 'collar feeling' done.

The reason for the head to repeatedly make his reference, was clearly because he thought by the ex-head boy becoming a policeman, it was a big deal. This may become more understandable when I tell you that there was a great tendency for teaching staff at the school to infer the majority of us pupils were going nowhere in life. Not once was I ever given homework, except punishment lines and one teacher I recall dared to say to the class, "What is the point, most of you, if you are lucky will go down the pit, the rest will be on the dole." It's little wonder with that attitude that the ex-head boy PC was regarded as having achieved something exceptionally great.

During one of the head's science lessons, I was shocked at something he did which ridiculed and humiliated a classmate, Ronnie Johnson, who had become a good friend of mine. He was very bright but his spelling ability was almost non-existent. Now dyslexia would have been recognised but back then you were just deemed to be thick. The head referred to Ronnie's poor spelling

39

and chalked on the blackboard what he had written in his exercise book, which was 'orl the peepl.' The class erupted with laughter. I felt for poor Ronnie but I never mentioned it to him because I did not know how to express my compassion back then. I have never forgotten how thoughtless and callous that was of the head.

After 55+ years I am now back in contact with, Ronnie and we have spoken via telephone. He remembered only too well, how the head had ridiculed him in front of the whole class. Ronnie told me that years later he was diagnosed as suffering from a form of dyslexia. I was pleasantly surprised and indeed flattered that after last seeing him so many years ago, he remembered my birthday as being the 14th of October, with his being 6 days earlier on the 8th. He said that every year he has toasted me on my birthday, having to frequently explain to his wife of nearly 50 years who I was.

Ronnie lived in Links Road at the bottom of my road. He has a younger brother Brian. Mr and Mrs Johnson were a lovely couple and Mrs Johnson was outstanding in her kindness and generosity. Ronnie's parents were one of the first to have a television. They opened up their home daily for years and invited kids in to view children's hour from 5 to 6 pm. Their lounge would be crowded and there would be kids squatting on the floor. My sister Kath being 7 years older acted as an honorary usherette and then spent the hour chatting in the kitchen with Mrs Johnson. I know they grew to be very fond of each other. At the end of the hour, Mrs Johnson would switch off, close the TV doors and drop a cloth down over the set, as many did back then. This indicated the show was over for that day and we all exited just as Mr Johnson arrived home from work. I reminded Ronnie of how much it meant that his Mam always so graciously welcomed us all into their home. I look forward to a reunion with Ronnie sometime in the future.

There was a female library teacher at the school who instilled fear into every kid she disapproved of. I'll call her Mrs Jones but many will know her true identity. Always with twinset, pearls and black wool coat, which she only ever draped over her shoulders and held together with her bony fingers. To my horror, it reminded me of Dracula's cape, as she prowled the cold corridors searching for her next victim and looking every bit like Margaret Rutherford playing a villain. She must have already had a birthday telegram from the Queen even back then! I'm still frightened to go into a library to this day, in case she swoops out at me!

I didn't even want her books but we were compelled to take them. I took them home and returned them a fortnight later without ever reading them. I even took the same books regularly because they were among a limited number that had pictures which I liked but she never picked up on that. I never even read books back then. All she ever taught me was to give a wide berth to any grumpy old battle-axe. As I am now 71 and single, that view seems to be somewhat diminishing my choices considering I reside in Hastings, where there are many old battle-axes of both types!

Another school chum was George Stanley. We were good pals nearly 60 years ago. He lost a library book and quite rightly he was dead scared of encountering Mrs Jones. He then took to being absent on our library day every fortnight. A pattern that I would have thought would have aroused early suspicion but surprisingly it did not.

I used to call on George every morning at his home in Holywell Crescent on the way to school and we'd walk together with his lovely kid sister Elizabeth. We would see her safely into the primary school. I recall I had to cover for George because he truanted, taking Elizabeth with him for company. I wouldn't go with him. I left them around by The Gut an open area of Amble and met up with them again after school to accompany them home just in case his parents' suspicions were aroused.

I was a good pal and covered for him and I never snitched. Surprisingly, he got away with it for months. Then I moved away to Darlington and I never heard the end. I fear he got caught as he surely could not have expected to evade capture forever. As you may imagine, I'm keen to hear how it ended. There is a sadness to this story and that is, no kid should have been so afraid of a teacher to take such drastic action. Unfortunately, in our day teachers frequently got away with it. Thankfully there were and still are more good teachers in the world than bad.

Sadly, I heard that Elizabeth got Alzheimer's at 49 and died at 59. She was a sweet delicate child and George was a very good protective brother. She was with us quite a bit and we never minded. Elizabeth will remain frozen in time in my memory, as that delightful little kid sister of my friend George. He could still be in hiding out in The Gut. I'll have to try and flush him out!

At the age of 13'ish, I recall the only outer jacket I had was a brown poor imitation leather zip jacket. I wore it because I did not have anything else not because I did not want to be smartly turned out in a black blazer with school badge, grey trousers, a white shirt and school tie. I did not from choice want to stand out from the norm, I had simply had no other choice. I was not eloquent enough at the age of 12-15 years to explain my position back then and I doubt that the teachers would have listened anyway. I and others were dealt with as if we were deliberately protesting against society and the establishment.

As soon I entered the school gates, I had been ordered to hand the jacket over to the headmaster's secretary and collect it at home time, as if I were using a cloakroom attendant facility, except no ticket was required because I was the only one out of hundreds of others, called upon to do it at that time. There were others at different periods who also had leather jackets but not at the same time as me. It did not even look like a leather jacket it was brown for a start and of a cheap plastic appearance. No self-respecting rocker would have worn such a thing but clearly, it was wrongly stigmatized as being an article of rebelliousness.

At least I avoided wearing hand me downs from my nearest sibling, who was my 7 years older sister, which might have proven to be more embarrassing than the jacket. Even worse, I overheard my Mam and her friend talking one day and her friend said, "There's some good stuff at the Army and Navy store. You never know they might have something that'll fit your Thomas?" I had a nightmare that night that very soon I could be going to school dressed as a Beefeater or a Japanese Admiral!

My footwear was always a headache to my parents, not only because of the cost but also the frequency they were required due to a kid's growing feet. Back then, if you were on social security and a school kid needed shoes or clothes, you made a claim and an officer came to your home to examine what you said needed replacing. Your claim was not always accepted but more times than not it was. At one time you were given a voucher for a clothing shop in Amble (there was only one) and you chose from their items.

I have been reminded frequently that when I was about 8 my Mam had a clothing voucher. When we visited the shop the owner said he had a little suit that came with 2 pairs of trousers but it was slightly more expensive than the voucher value. My Mam was convinced it was a good buy because she knew the trousers always became unserviceable before the jacket and so I should get double wear out of the suit. She scraped together the extra and away we went. However, it did not work out quite as she planned because I ripped the back out of, not the trousers but the jacket getting under a barbed-wire fence whilst taking a shortcut. So I didn't have a little suit anymore but I still had 2 pairs of trousers.

It always seemed to me that I was in the wrong seasonal footwear sandshoes (plimsolls) in the winter and wellingtons in the summer. Now I must make it clear that these were not in addition to everyday shoes, they were instead of. If only we could miss a season it would correct itself, I must have thought. I remember

44

very clearly being given a letter stating the school's requirements regarding footwear. Probably it stays with me because I had no prospect whatsoever of having any of them, never mind all.

This is what I read, soft-soled shoes for hall morning prayers, sandshoes for the gymnasium, football boots and I especially remember the last, 'sensible shoes' in the classroom. I was confused as to what were sensible shoes. Looking down at mine for any glimmer of inspiration and seeing the sole coming away from the upper and flapping about as if somehow laughing at me, I decided sadly they were definitely not the sensible shoes I needed! Mine were definitely what I'd call un-sensible shoes! However, the rules were relaxed for me and there were others in the same unfortunate boat because we were allowed to go anywhere with whatever we happened to be strutting our stuff in at the time. Much the same as in the army if you are excused boots.

I had quite severe asthma and I was prescribed inhalers at a very early age and it prevented me from enthusiastically taking part in any school sports. Cross country runs were a total nightmare and to a lesser degree, all the others were too. Many times I was forced by the sports teacher into full participation. It was commonly known that I had breathing problems but they either did not understand how debilitating it was or they just thought it was a put-on. I was genuinely quite badly affected and both psychology and allergy can trigger an attack. Only a sufferer can fully understand how distressing it can be. I got around it by, for example, in football, I would be the goalkeeper or if on the field I'd just sort of hang about. Cross country runs I would just walk and arrive back when it was getting dark and just in the nick of time before the police were called! I seemed to be able to manage a small burst of energy but could not sustain it but I was never what you would call a sprinter. Oh! No, the nearest I ever got to being a cheetah was when I got caught copying in a maths lesson!

Besides my asthma, I was never going to excel at sports, especially football because I often played in wellingtons. When that was the case, on seeing my footwear the kids picking the teams would always leave me to the very last. The unlucky team that got to pick second of course always got me. It might come as a surprise that on one occasion when I found myself playing and not in goal, I did attack goal and put one past the goalkeeper. Sadly, I was not hailed as a one-off hero of that game because the goal was disallowed, on what I still maintain, to be a harsh technicality.

This is what happened. I was just sort of hanging about as usual, which was only ever my tactic. I happened to be in the goal-mouth when the ball fell right at my feet. Imagining, I was Bobby Lightfoot, I smashed it with my right foot and with such force, the back of the net was nearly taken off. Alas, there was to be no glory that day or any other on a football field for me because what happened was, it was my wellington that whizzed past the goalie and hit the back of the net. The football went off in a different direction! I found there was a big bonus playing in wellingtons in that I did not have to change them or undo laces to clean them. A quick swill under the outside tap and I was ready for the next classroom lesson.

I feared the school sports day but I did have the presence of mind to fake an asthma attack on that day each year. It would take a long time for the pattern to be spotted because there is only one a year and only a handful of years of senior school life. I believe that if you follow that simple plan it is almost undetectable and therefore foolproof. It was the track events that worried me this time more than the cross country run, that was simple I would just as usual walk it. The problematical events to me were the long jump, high jump and especially the hurdles.

Have you ever tried hurdling whilst wearing wellingtons? Well, it is a lot harder than the long jump and the high jump, I can tell you. The only way that hurdling in wellingtons could have been any harder, would have been if my Mam had failed to cut the string that tied the pair together when they were bought. We were told that with the right amount of training and work dedication, you too can win an Olympic medal. In my case, that was just not going to happen. Well, not until they change the rules at the Paralympics and have an event of hurdling for asthmatics, whilst wearing wellingtons!

Many teachers had no idea what it was like to be poor and to go without. Little thought went into how a kid could be embarrassed or hurt by their thoughtlessness and lack of understanding. For example, most of my school life I got free school dinners but I felt ashamed that was the case. I wanted the dinners and was very grateful for them. I never whined about the quality or bothered about eating for example tapioca. I recall when it was on the menu a cry would go up of, 'Yuk! Frogspawn.' I thought lovely bring it on,

I'll get seconds today. I loved custard and prunes, except when I noticed that I always very oddly, got SIX prunes. I started to suspect they were a plant. As for the other kids who did the tinker, tailor, soldier etc. count, I just absolutely refused to join in!

The free school milk and dinners are what partly kept me interested in school some of the time and they were a big attendance incentive to me. Marcus Rashford the young footballer is to be applauded for his current campaign for free school meals. Please do not get the impression that I am saying I was on a par with Oliver Twist. My parents gave me what they could but it was less than most. I was an adult when I remembered that my Mam gave to me, whilst often saying she was not hungry. The school meals varied menu and quality was a treat to me. Although I appreciated the free meals, what I did not appreciate was another part of it.

I am talking about a time here in the 50s/60s, when school meals were one shilling per day (5p. now) and thus 5 shillings per week. Monday morning after the attendance register was called, it was then the turn of the dinner register and what followed would be similar to this; The teacher being out front in a loud voice would call out, "Andrews, 5 shillings." Andrews being male or female would go to the teacher and hand over their cash and sit down. Then, "Brown 4 shillings, you were absent 1-day last week, so you have one shilling credit." Brown would hand over his money, then, "Curry free" and then, "Dawson 5 shillings" and so on.

Was it really necessary to shout out, 'Curry free?' If I was eligible for free meals, I knew that and there was no need to announce it
48

to the whole class every week. It was shouted out that often I began to think I had a double-barrelled surname, i.e. Curry-Free! Each time I heard that it was like a sword to my heart but dignity back then especially that of a kid was overlooked. Did these so-called educated people not stop and think that a child could be caused embarrassment?

Do not forget that back then teachers got away with rapping your knuckles with a ruler, throwing chalk and blackboard rubbers in your direction, to startle and cause fear and were officially and legally licensed to beat you with specifically manufactured leather belts and canes and without the prior knowledge or presence of parents. How barbaric that sounds now and it doesn't seem as if we had advanced a great deal since the bloody Tudor times, does it? Never mind the 'good old days' some things were far from good but thank goodness and good riddance to such behaviour, I say!

THE MYSTERIOUS BOX

The next tale is one I view as being quite funny, which I find refreshingly detracts my attention from any sadness within. Our lady form teacher, I'll call her Miss Greenway, made the following announcement, "To keep the desktops tidy and to contain your pens and pencils etc. I want everyone to have their own pencil case. Those who do not already have one, I have some for sale for 6 pennies." (2½ p. now) I must have thought, 'Here we go again!' She continued, "For those of you who cannot afford that, are you listening, Curry? You may as an alternative bring a cardboard box in to be used in place of a pencil case. I will write the dimensions it must be on the board. Copy them down and measure the box before bringing it to school."

At home, I told my Mam the teacher's instructions. There then ensued with much shaking of the head and sighing something which I had heard from her many times which went something like this, "I don't know where that school thinks I can get all the money from and they know your Dad's not working. I've got a round bum but I can't poo money." I've altered two words of a more colourful language but you have to remember where we are, i.e. NE coal mining village and not leafy upmarket Buckinghamshire.

I set to in search of a suitable box. It was not going to be easy as there was not the amount of packaging about as there is today. I was just on the verge of giving up when as a last throw of the dice I found one that might do the job. I checked the measurements and it was good. I put it in my bedroom and put a few bits and pieces in it including some pencils. The next day I set off for school with it tucked under my arm. I would not have a pencil case but at least what I did have would satisfy Miss Greenway. So as normal, I walked via the main streets to school.

When it was time, I entered and walked along the corridor. Suddenly, I heard a voice shout, "Curry, come here?" It was Mr Whitlow and he was not looking pleased. I thought what could it be, I was not running, talking, chewing or doing anything wrong, as far as I knew. He said, "What have you got that for?" meaning the box. I said, "For my pencils, sir." He said, "For your pencils?" I said, "Yes sir, Miss Greenway said I had to bring a box in." "Give me
50

that," he said and snatched it from me. He tipped the contents onto the ground and said, "Pick them up and get along." He quickly tucked the box inside his jacket and walked off. Talk about confused, I could not understand what had upset him but I could not do anything about it. So there I was, no pencil case and now no box.

I went to my classroom and a short while later Miss Greenway asked who had boxes. She came to me and said, "Where's yours?" I said, "I did have one but Mr Whitlow took it." She said, "What, and why did Mr Whitlow take it?" I said, "I don't know miss?" "Well, what were you doing with it?" "Nothing, miss", I said. She said, "You better be telling me the truth because I shall see Mr Whitlow about it." So that was that for the time being.

Surprisingly Miss Greenway did not say anything until I asked her if she had spoken to Mr Whitlow nearing home time. She said, "Yes, I have and I'm telling you now that if I ever hear you mention that box again to anyone you will be in big trouble. Do you understand?" and pointed her finger at me. I understood what she said but I did not know exactly why everyone was so upset about a box.

Over time I forgot all about it. Then many years later something triggered my thought process and I remembered the incident. Being older and wiser, it suddenly dawned on me what it was all about. I deliberately did not give any detail as to where I found the box or describe it. I found it in the airing cupboard semi-concealed amongst the linen. I opened it and I thought, 'Ok I'll just leave these bandages inside on the shelf.' I put the box in my bedroom and the next morning I went off with it and my parents did not see me leave with it.

I had walked all the way to school along the main streets with a Dr White's sanitary towel box tucked under my arm. It's little wonder it was snatched from me and I was threatened with secrecy. Don't forget this was in the early 60s when such things were not discussed and were not on open display. There were no supermarkets or self-service back then.

I can recall being with my Mam or sisters and them being served. They would lean forward and whisper. The shopkeeper would go under the counter and wrap something in newspaper and quickly pass it over and it would be shoved into the shopping bag. I might say, "What's that?" and I would be told, "Nothing for little boys!" If anything is sure to capture a kid's attention and curiosity it is that odd and furtive behaviour. As adults, I spoke to my sister about it and blamed her. We laughed about it for years!

SCHOOL TRIPS

I remember at one time there were 3 school trips on offer at the same time, a Mediterranean cruise, a weekend in Paris and a trip to Newcastle to see a pantomime.

I recall my cousin, Richard told me he was going on the cruise. Don't overlook the fact that this was 1962'ish, so it was not cheap. Richard was an only child and his father was my Uncle Roland, Mam's brother. Richard appeared to have everything and was well turned out in his school uniform. I think him speaking to me was only to tell me that his name was down for the cruise because we rarely spoke, although there could have been many opportunities when we could have done so. I did not envy him and we would have had little in common.

I was amazed when my Mam told me to put my name down for the Paris trip, which I did. If it amazed me it would have shocked the teachers. I cannot recall it but it sounds like maybe, my Dad might have again been briefly, back at the pit. At school, weekly instalment payments were started but much the same pattern emerged as in the case of any HP agreement, they began to be missed and then came to a halt. The amounts deposited were of a pittance and the shortfall meant the situation had become desperate.

Eventually, after being frequently reminded of the shortfall by the teacher, there came a time when I had to say that I could not afford to go. I cannot remember being crestfallen, as I was no softie. I had become, through frequency, accustomed to taking a knockback and it was nothing new to me.

I was pretty streetwise and well known for my quick wit and humour, even as a kid. The only difficulty I may have had was not having it totally under control at certain times when seriousness was the order of the day. I can now admit that it could have, on occasions, been a distraction in class but normally it was appreciated both by pupils and staff alike. Only one or two teachers during my school life did not appreciate my humour or indeed my upbeat fun-loving character but on the whole, the great majority appeared to like me. This proved to be correct as the date of the Paris trip came closer but it had long since become of no further interest to me. I had paid no attention to any reference to it, as it no longer involved me.

One day I was summoned to see the headmaster, Mr Johnstone and as any kid would be, I was apprehensive. It could be for a multitude of reasons, was it the lack of school uniform, my habit of being late, a wisecrack making the class laugh or maybe something I could not even think of. I had the cane from him only once for some minor misdemeanour and I was not wildly enthusiastic about renewing that acquaintance again.

So in I went and I saw that the head was behind his desk. (Just the head, no body, no arms, no legs!) I thought what may be about to come was his frequently used, when addressing the school assembly, speech i.e. 'You have let your parents down, you have let us, teachers down, you've let the school down and worst of all you have let the whole of Amble down!' Whenever I heard him say that, I had a vision that the whole of Amble, including all the people, were made of inflated rubber and I was running amok with a pin!

This time the head seemed to be in one of his rare amiable moods and he instructed me to sit down, I was still on my guard as I thought it could be a trick or he thought I was someone else but then I remembered he told me once that he would keep an eye on me and would not forget me. For a long time after that, I also kept an eye on him, checking to see that his eye was not on me!

He said, "If you still want to, you can go on the Paris trip." I said, "I can't sir, we can't afford it." He said, "You don't have to, the teachers and I have decided you can go and you do not have to pay." I was confused and said, "Who's going to pay for me, then?" He said, "Don't you worry about that. We're going to sort that out. Are you happy?" I found myself saying, "No, sir." He said, "Why not?" I said, "Because I don't want to go if I can't pay." He said, "Why not?" I said, "Because I don't want charity, sir."

I have over the years regretted saying that, as it sounds so ungrateful and undiplomatic but at that age, I was still a kid and had not yet developed any people skills. The head tried to persuade me to take the offer but I had made my mind up and my pride would not allow it. I have always been the same in that regard if I cannot pay my way then count me out. He gave me time saying, "Speak to your parents." I did and they said, "Go" but that still did not change my mind. I realised much later, what an extremely kind and generous gesture it was. It authenticated the fact that after all, I must have been liked by the teaching staff.

As a consolation and with the help of my brother Alan I did get to go on the cheapest trip i.e. Newcastle pantomime. At the last minute, I discovered part of the sole of one of my shoes was coming away. We had a cobblers metal shoe last at home and so my Dad got it on there and ripped part of the sole off and knocked the nails back down with a hammer but he couldn't get them right down flat for fear of ruining the shoe altogether. The only thing I can remember about the whole trip is the shoe nails were catching on the carpet in the theatre foyer as I walked across it. At one stage they were picking up discarded lolly papers and I began to get taller but lopsided. Other kids pointed it out to me but not wanting to reveal why it was happening, I just said, "Cobblers!"

Throughout my childhood, even though money was tight and I saw what other kids were given, I had a strange habit of refusing any pocket money from anyone outside my direct family, when someone wanted to give me something, including my uncles and aunties. On many occasions, my Uncle Joe would try to give me a couple of bob as a treat but I would never accept it. If at his home, he would force it on me but he would discover it on the arm of the sofa or such like when I'd left. He'd say to my Mam, "Wat's rang wi wor Thomas. He winnit tak owt from is ya na?" I was never persuaded to change on that score. I accepted a Christmas present of course but that was never given face to face.

The only time I can remember getting pocket money on any regular basis was from about the age of 9 for a couple of years, until Ray left home for Worthing. My brother had a wage increase and he began to give me half a crown (12 ½ p) when he got paid on a Friday. He would make me think I was earning it by giving me the shoes he was going to wear that night to clean, as he was getting ready. They were always clean but I'd take them downstairs and my Dad would buff them up and then I'd take them back to Ray.

AMBLE/NE PIT HUMOUR

I want to share with you stories about my Dad and my Uncle Joe, which may illustrate the type of men our forebears were, especially those who worked, 'doon the pit'.

My Uncle Joe lived happily in Amble all his life and never wanted to be anywhere else. He lived in St. Cuthbert's Ave., just he and my Granny. After Granny Purvis died and Joe was in his 40s, he married a fantastic lovely lady, Bet Clark and they continued to live in the same house with their daughter, Brenda. Bet was as witty as Joe and so they were a great match. They were very happy together for many years. Bet died before Joe and he went on to marry Tess Caruthers and they lived in a bungalow, still in Amble. They too were equally as happy but this time, Joe predeceased Tess.

My Uncle Joe was a pitman all his working life. He was a tough but reserved man and was well respected. I never once saw him down and never did I hear him complain about his lot. He seemed happy to get by on a pitman's wage and his coal ration and he remained in council property throughout his life. He was simply a very nice uncomplicated man who was happy leading a simple life and without a lot of the frills we enjoy today, as were the majority back then.

Joe had a typical Amble pitman's humour and sharp wit, my Dad had too but to a lesser extent. He was even more reserved than his brother in law. Joe and Dad loved nothing more than sharing a joke. They both would regale us young 'uns with tall tales and they thought it was great to verbally entertain with their yarns and wildly exaggerated pit humour.

I will share with you a couple of such tall tales so that you may get an indication of what I mean and it may well remind you if you too have experienced similar pit humour.

On one occasion that I will never forget, Joe whilst telling what it was like to work down Hauxley pit elaborated with the following; He said that he was one of the best workers down the pit,(true but not to the extent of what follows,) as such he was tasked with working all day pick-axing. He was told that he had to get a move on as they had to get ahead with the coalface and pronto! Joe said, "I really got a lick on, an wat wi the speed the pick-axe was gannin, it waz nowt but a blur. An al day ya na, an in wetter up ta me chin but wat a had'nt realised waz, az weel az gannin forard, I was gannin upwards tee, an ta such an extent that, wey man, suddenly a hord an awful rumblin soond up aheight, an a thought what the hell's that? An a waz just waitin for a cave-in. Wey al of a sudden ya bugga ma, the bloody shurt (shirt) was ripped clean offa me back, a was lucky that day cos a gota way wi nowt, not even a scratch or owt!"

Wey, wat it was, was Bobby Forsyth (who farmed from where the Granary, Amble is now) was plowin his field wi ees tractor and it waz the plow that had ripped the shurt ofa me back. Wey by lad hoo that plow mist me al niver na." I believed that for years!

Another time my Dad told me that a pitman was biking home on his own from the pit at about 2/3 in the morning. Just as he passed the cemetery at the bottom of Links Ave. a ghost swooped out from under the steeple arch (spookier then because the street lighting was poor) and came for him. My Dad went on, "Wey he doon on tha bike pedals lad but just then his chain came off. He was so frightened and he pedalled so fast, he still got yem (home) to the top end of Amble or the ghost wada had im lad. Aye, he waz lucky that night!"

Well honestly now, not only did that scare the wits out of me but what made it worse was the cemetery was only at the bottom of our street. For years I made sure I never went past there after dark. I also wondered why my bike would still not go if the chain came off and I pedalled as fast as I could, even when told it would not by other kids. I merely said, "My Dad says it will but it might be just only when a ghost comes after you."

Here's a joke my Dad called his 'pit joke.' There was a family of snakes and one day the baby snake came home crying. The daddy snake said, "Wat's rang wi ee?" The baby snake said, "The Smith's won't let me hiss in their pit." The daddy snake said, "I knew the Smith's when they didn't have a pit to hiss in!"

My Uncle Joe was in an Amble pub one time and from afar, without being noticed, he over-heard another pitman who he knew, telling a group this; "I was in the garden today and I saw an unusual burd, it was like a blackburd but it had a pure white heed. A divent na wat (I don't know what) it waz but it wasn't from aroond here an might of been blown off course." A healthy debate then ensued but it appeared the listeners were not convinced. i.e. "Waz it a magpie." Reply, "No, ower big, an it's gotta black heed."

Later Joe moved to the bar and one of the group said, "Hoos it gannin Joe, wat fettle? Wat ya been up tu?" Joe replied, "Av spent al day paintin sumit an a peculiar thing happened. (the group stopped and listened.) He continued," Wey a waz painten outside and a got sum paint on me troosers an so I went indoors an got some white spirit an when I came ootside again, a hurd an arful screechin soond an a looked up an 2 blackburds were up aheight an each had hold of an end of a worm tha were fighten ower . Wey as tha were flyin tha must of both let go an tha worm fell and it dropped right inta the pot of white paint I'd left on the patio. Quick as a flash one of the burds swooped doon stuck its heed right in tha paint pot and pulled oot tha worm an flew off wi it. Its heed waz covered in tha white paint." There was a gasp and the victim broke the silence by shouting, "There ya ar a told ya al I saw that burd Joe. Wey ya bugga ma, I saw it today, an al!"

A rod fisherman pitman mate told Joe that once that he'd caught a conger eel from Amble pier and it was 6 feet long. Joe said nothing at the time but remembered it weeks later in another conversation with the same feller. Joe said that at the pit he'd dropped his naked flame carbide lamp and it fell to the ground and disappeared down into 2 feet of standing water. (not uncommon for that amount and more.) He grabbed the lamp so quick from down in the water that surprisingly the flame was still alight. After some humming and harring, the victim said, "Na come off it Joe, noo ya divent expect is ta believe that dee you?" Joe replied, "Oh wey ya can plees yersel like but al tell ya wat, if ee knock 5 foot offa ya eel, I'll blo the flame on tha lamp oot!"

60

Joe was never unkind to man nor beast and an indication of this is the photo of him with an eider duck and the story that follows.

He loved nothing better than to walk along the Amble beaches. I was with him 30+ years ago on the Links beach. An eider duck was badly entangled in fishing line. Joe sprung into action, soon catching the poor duck. A halt was called to the walk and we returned hotfoot to Anne Crescent with the duck and Joe took it to a lady somewhere nearby who cared for birds saying, "She'll git it loose without frettin it." Once free, we returned to the exact same spot on the beach to happily release the poor duck, which then turned into a lucky duck. Nowhere else would do and my young nephews were not allowed to go near the duck.

Uncle Joe and the lucky duck.

A well known local Amblite Andy Capp type character, who never did work was the butt of many amusing stories. Some undoubtedly he was wrongly credited with but on the whole, they were true. I will let you decide which have any merit. Many will still remember him as a small quick-witted and full of confidence dapper man, except for the fact he always wore a pair of old and grubby off white sandshoes, (plimsolls) which he merely blackened over with boot polish when he gave his daughter away on the day of her wedding. I will describe him no further out of respect to any remaining relatives

The dole office was at the top end of Amble and in those days opposite Gino's fish and chip shop. Our guy lived at the bottom end. Joe said that our guy always went to the front of any waiting dole queue saying, "Howay, mek (make) room for the regulars," irrespective of their size. The officer at the dole office once said to him, "Don't you expect me to pay you out. I saw you on the back of the coal lorry!" "Aye", our man said, "an a sar ee on tha bus but you wernt dishin oot tha tickets." Joe swore this was true as was this, he saw him in Queen's St. one day and said to him, "Hoo doo. Hey, I've just read tha ganna bring tha dole money doon." As quick as a flash he said, "Thank God fur that am sick a gannin al tha way up there fur it!"

You got 3 green cards from the dole office in those days to go for a job interview. If you didn't go the dole money got stopped. Our guy, never got an offer of work because everyone knew he was a little waster. On one occasion it was said, he was sent to Hauxley pit and the Manager said, "As long as I live, I'll never give you a job." Without hesitation, he responded by saying, "Long may you live, sir. Good day to you." That was enough for him. He'd complied with the green card.

He used to pinch coal off the railway wagons at the rear of St. Cuthbert's Ave. (Wor Gladys' patch) where Uncle Joe lived. He'd leave his bike outside the front of some house or other. He'd fill his sack from a wagon, hop over the fence of the house and put it on his bike, to give the impression he'd got it from that house, even though you weren't supposed to sell or give your coal away. He had the cheek of the devil and one time Joe arrived home and saw the bike outside his house and here he is walking down Joe's path with a sack. Joe said, "Wat du ee want?" He said, Err, does Mr (and said a name) live here?" Joe said, "Givower man ee na av lived here al ma life."

It was said the police caught him once pinching coal but he was given a caution because he was selling it to some of the copper's wives! Unlike the majority of Amble folk, they were not employed by the NCB and therefore did not get a free coal allowance.

AMBLE PICTURE HOUSE

As a kid, Amble only had the 'picture house' (NE never said, cinema) and the only way to tell what was on was by looking at the board outside or word of mouth. For years Uncle Joe had the same replies if asked what was on. His grandkids would have been likely spared this next piece, as sadly it closed. It always followed the same script whoever asked, year in year out, you either got one of the replies but generally all 3 as follows;

Q.... What's on at the pictures? R...The roof. Q.... No, come on? R... It's Tarzan SWIMS the desert. Q.....Do you know? R....Aye, a dee. It's, The Flyers, starring Gregory Peck, Walter Pigeon and Anna Neagle! (All were actual actors of the day.) Q.....Do you know or not? R.... No, a divent. Hoo du ya think a shud na, like? All the many frustrating times but how I wish I could hear him respond, just one more time.

Joe used to repeatedly tell a joke whenever the picture house was mentioned. Although it was well past its sell-by date, it is still amusing but only if you understand which era it comes from and what was happening at that time at the picture houses. Cinema (or theatre) organs made music for silent films in the 1920s but when talkies were released they took on the role of solo musical instruments. Cinema-goers would often find the music of the Mighty Wurlitzer or Compton and Christie, just as exciting as the film and the organists themselves became stars. Often the organs were stored below floor level and would silently move up and down using an electrical lift, just before the start of any performance.

I think that is enough information to understand the joke but of course, Joe would never give a prologue he would just launch into it. I never knew him to go to the cinema and so he either thought it was the same as the 20s or he assumed you knew what he was talking about. Phew!

So finally here is the joke. A man went to the picture house to see a particular film he'd wanted to see for a very long time. To get the best seat in the house, 2 hours before the start and in the pouring rain, he was first in the queue and therefore first through the door. He hurried in and sat in a seat right at the front of the screen. Just before the film started a man tapped him on the shoulder and said, "You're in my seat!" The seated man said, "Luk, I've queued 2 oors in tha pouring rain to get the best seat in the hoose and I'm not moving." "Ok", said the other man, "when the organ comes up, you play it!"

10 YR. OLD, BANNED FROM THE PICTURE HOUSE

A can recall being ejected and banned from the picture house on one occasion. It was around about 1959 and I was about 10. I know this because I remember the film that was about to start, that being South Pacific. It was released in 1958 but it seemed that films never reached Amble until the rest of the world had seen them. Amble was taken aback and amazed when 'talkies' came out there in 1980. Only joking! Sadly Amble picture house closed and it became a bingo hall in about 1965. My sister Kath, who would be 17, had taken me to the picture house on this occasion. A practice by kids at the time was to throw their empty ice cream and drink cartons upwards into the light overhead of the film being projected on to the screen, from the projectionists opening at the rear. This does not happen now in the digital age. The shadow of the container would show on the screen, which was thought by the kids to be a neat trick. This act was more prolific at a Saturday kids matinee performance. The matinees were bedlam anyway and to have tried to police the many such antics would have been impossible and therefore it continued unabated.

However, Kath and I were at an evening performance and such acts were rare and therefore easier to both detect and deter. So after the interlude and just as South Pacific was about to begin, I had consumed my ice cream and without prior warning, I repeated the container trick. Only, I had not taken into account the fact we were seated right at the front and the container not only went up but was also propelled forwards too. It narrowly missed hitting the screen by a fine margin and fell just short onto the front of the stage. A torch beam was directed onto us and we both were escorted out. With no further ado, we were ejected having been told that I was now banned until I had learnt my lesson and could refrain from such behaviour. It was emphasised, "If that had hit the screen it would have had to be replaced costing hundreds of pounds and your parents would be responsible for the cost."

What I didn't think of saying at the time, was that if they were lucky they might get a shilling a week for the first couple of weeks and then one of my Mam's famous, 'You can't get blood out of a stone letters.' Very fairly, Kath was told that did not apply to her. I haven't been back as yet because I'm not altogether convinced I can give any such guarantee that I can behave myself but maybe that will happen in the future when I'm a bit older!

Seriously though, after some time had passed, a guarantee was given, together with a large dose of pleading by lovely Kath on my behalf and the extremely gracious Mr & Mrs Aitchison (managers) allowed me to return. My family and I were appreciative of their kind gesture because the pictures played a big part in Amble's entertainment back then, as there was nothing much else at that time. As an example of its importance, years later I was still pointed out as the kid who nearly brought an end to the silver screen, in Amble anyway!

I attended whenever I could, often seeing the same film. It's little wonder that I can recognise film stars from that era but not those of now. I do not attend cinemas now but perhaps my conduct helped to bring about the end of rear-projected films. If I did go, maybe it would be prudent for me to bypass any refreshments. By the way, I never have seen South Pacific. Maybe if I ever learn to behave, I'll finally get to see it, eh?

FILM STAR GREGORY PECK

In 1973 I was to come face to face with the fantastic film actor Gregory Peck, the butt of Uncle Joe's, 'The Flyers' joke. I had been a great fan of his ever since seeing his 1956 classic film, Moby Dick when he played the part of Captain Ahab, who was obsessed with hunting the white whale.

I had been to see Frank Sinatra in his 'Ol' Blue Eyes Is Back' concert tour, at the Royal Festival Hall, with the Count Basie Orchestra. I had left the theatre and I was about to cross the road. A tall distinguished man standing next to me stepped onto the road in front of a Rolls Royce, which was pulling away. I shouted, "Look out" and he quickly stepped back onto the kerb. He must have forgotten that here in the UK we drive on the left.

I recognised him instantly as being the great man himself, Gregory Peck. (I don't think he recognised me!) He said, "Thank you." Apparently, he was a big buddy of Frank Sinatra and he must have been to the show. Instead of 'Look out,' I should have shouted what the lookout shouted in Moby Dick, "Tha she blows!" He moved away too quickly for me to tell him Uncle Joe's joke or to ask if he really was in the film, The Flyers?

Yes, folks, I'm the guy who saved the late great, Gregory Peck, TWICE. First from an accident and second from relating Uncle Joe's The Flyers, joke!

A MYSTERY TOUR TO SOMEWHERE UNKNOWN

A funny thing happened to Uncle Joe once involving a coach trip. (Bus trip, in the NE) He and his wife always were enthusiastic about going on such trips. They went to the midlands on a short break and whilst there they decided they wanted to go on one. So they found that there was a mystery tour planned for the following day and so thinking that would be enjoyable, two seats were paid for and duly booked. They always enjoyed the adventure of a mystery tour but that was to prove not to be the case in this instance. I guess as normal they were excited as they took their seats and the chat would likely have been, "I wonder where we're going, eh?" as the bus headed northwards, instead of the hoped-for south.

Well, it was to get a great deal worse because one of the destinations and stops was to be back to their hometown of Amble and that is exactly where they found themselves. So

68

making the best of a bad job they went home, checked the house, post, made a cup of tea and when it was time they got back on the bus. Joe laughed about it of course and said that if they had taken their cases with them they would have forsaken the last two days and just stopped at home. He did have the presence of mind to say, "Tha winnit be any mare mystery toors fur us if tha not booked from Amble," which of course made perfect sense. He did finish by saying, "Keep it ta yersel mind and divent broadcast it." So, shhh!

Uncle Joe as I mentioned was a quiet reserved man and never nasty. Even though he was mild-mannered, by a disapproving look or a point of the finger, he could halt even an adult, if he thought you had gone far enough. I guess he achieved that by being a man of few words and perhaps that is why what he did say is remembered with ease. Do not get me wrong he was no mute but he did not enter into idle chit chat or malicious gossip. He loved a joke or a yarn. He was very approachable and indeed sociable as can be gathered by my many quotes but most of the time he was content listening, as opposed to being the centre of attention. He was kind and thoughtful and very well-liked and respected in Amble. He went to work and was conscientious and was the perfect build and size for a pitman, not too tall but stocky and powerfully built. The ideal pitman it was said should be as broad as he was tall.

Both my brothers went down the pit and they were well over 6 feet tall and they found life underground very difficult indeed.

They would have undoubtedly suffered health-wise later in life had they not moved on to different occupations.

THE COALFACE

(For those who are not aware, a coalface is an exposed surface of coal in a mine.)

Joe did a bit of pier fishing and he liked his garden and home. He was a reliable and genuine husband and father to Brenda. He was not bothered ever about pubs or alcohol but very occasionally he would partake in a glass of beer.

In the early 50s, there was an occasion when Joe found himself in a bad situation and if left unaddressed, it may have escalated into something serious. Joe took control instantly and it was quelled.

My Uncle Tom, 'Wor Gladys' husband, often took a beer or two. He liked to argue but heated debating perhaps would be a better description. However, he was not aggressive in the slightest. He was in a local pub and a disagreement took place with a local well-known man, Tommy ? who decided he was going to sort out Tom, with a broken beer bottle.

Tom was then in his late 40s and fighting was not for him. So he decided to take off with Tommy in hot pursuit. Instead of running home, at least he was thinking straight. Bypassing his own house, he ran on further to Granny Purvis' home, where he knew his brother Joe would be indoors.

The back door at Granny P's was always unlocked. Tom opened the door and leaning on it once inside, kept it from being opened

70

again. He was met by Joe, with a small fireside shovel in his hand. Joe said to the panting Tom, "Wat tha hell's a matter wi ee?" To which Tom said, "Divent gan oot there. Tommy ? is after is an ees got a broken beer bottle." Joe gently moved Tom out of the way, whilst saying, "A divent care if Tommy ? has a Tommy gun. A want a shull a coal." Joe opened the door to find the said Tommy, with a broken bottle in hand, on the doorstep. Joe instantly, with the flat of the coal shovel, walloped him straight in the face. There was a loud 'boinggg' sound and Tommy fell backwards into the doorless coal bunker opposite. Joe and Tom helped Tommy, his face blackened, down into the street and he thanked them both before departing. Now Granny P had heard the noise but not what was said and she had looked out the front window to see the 3 of them and that Tommy was being supported off the premises.

Granny enquired, "Wat's gannin on?" to be told that Tommy and Tom had come to see Joe about something and Tommy had one of his dizzy turns. Granny P never knew the truth. What I think is amusing is that the 2 middle-aged tough pitmen were still concerned that their tiny old Mam should not know the truth and she never would. Joe and Tom never had any more bother from Tommy after that, other people did but they did not. Often Tom would say something like, "I saw the coalface the day" (today) but Joe always said, "Forget it, man." Joe was not one to hold a grudge or crow about anything.

GRANNY PURVIS

Granny Purvis, as aforementioned, had brought up my 7 uncles and aunties alone, after being sadly widowed at a young age. My Uncle Joe lived with her in their 3-bed council house and Joe was well into his forties when she passed away. I do not think Joe ever paid a fixed amount of board. He simply put his hard-earned wages in a drawer and Granny took whatever she needed. That was Joe's decision not demanded by Granny. She was not an ogre and we all loved and respected her in equal amounts.

Granny Purvis.

Right to the day she left this world, she was treated with respect and courtesy by all of the family. She was a tiny woman barely 5' as I recall but with the inner strength and heart of a lion. She quietly ruled the roost to her end and her word went. No, ifs or buts, that was it! I cannot remember Granny doing much other than being indoors and going to the local bingo. She did not smoke or drink or go away on holidays.

A command I never looked forward to was, "Come on, wa gannin to see Granny." I knew then that called for me to be on my very best behaviour with no larking about for sure. Granny had her rules and you were all too frequently reminded of them. Such as, 'Little boys don't interrupt when grown-ups are tarkin' but that seemed to mean nothing because if I spoke when they were not, she would say, "Little boys should be seen and not hurd." I had to sit in one place and if I moved I was told, "Av ee got tha worms laddie? Al give ee a dose a cod liver oil." Throughout WW2 rationing, cod liver oil was given out free to pre-school kids by the National Health Service, together with orange juice. The former was foul but it still did not stop it from being shoved into kids. If I even dreamed of touching anything I was told, "Little boys shud see al and touch nowt." If my Mam went to say something maybe controversial, Granny would say, "Hey remember wor Emma, wals have ears." I'd maybe look around at the walls and Granny would say, "It's ee wa takin aboot, yur tha wal!"

RAY HOTFOOTS IT, AFTER ME!

I was an exceptionally mischievous child but not out of control, quite the contrary because my Mam would have quickly stamped on that, for she had many of her Mam's traits. I was always telling jokes or up to pranks, such as hiding in cupboards and jumping out at people irrespective of their age or you might find a dead mouse in your shoe. I drove them all nuts because there was just no let-up.

The worst thing I did was when I was only about 10. My brother Ray was about 20. He had been drinking Sunday lunchtime and was having a nap on the top of his bed and he did not have any socks on. I must have been temporarily possessed by the devil because I put a match between his toes, lit it and ran away. My poor brother ran/hopped 'hotfoot' after me and he had every right to knock the hell out of me and he did but that was the only time. Needless to say, there has never been a 'rematch'!

I must have been influenced by The Three Stooges or Tom & Jerry or something because they never appeared injured. Did they? If they were, it was not for long. A kid might think like that, maybe.

My Dad never laid a hand on me but my Mam hit me with everything, broom handles, coat hangers, belts, sticks or anything she had in her hand at the time, she would let fly with it. It must have worked because the police were never at our door even though we had very little. Mam used to repeatedly say, "If you see a pin on the ground and it's not yours you do not pick it up. If the police ever come here for you, you will not be coming back here again." Yes, Mam had a bit of Granny in her, for her 5 of a brood never got into any real trouble either.

I can remember getting a good hiding from Mam for telling this joke, 'What did the mouse say to the cat?' Reply, 'Come around the corner and I'll show you my hole.' I'd overheard my sister Kath telling it to her friends and getting a laugh and so I tried it. I didn't get a laugh but I got something I hadn't bargained on. Kath denied it. I was about 10 and didn't even understand what the joke meant but I knew it got a laugh and that's what mattered to me then. I remember crying and saying, 'The hole in the wall.'

MORTON'S CAFE AND THE MORTON FAMILY

Another place that played a big part in our Amble life was a shop at the bottom of our street on Links Road, adjacent to the southwest corner of the cemetery, called Morton's Cafe. In fact in the 50s and early 60s, I never knew it to be a cafe as such, only as a general store. It was a dark brown wooden structured hut type building and was originally the Links Golf Clubhouse sited at Panhaven Road and opened in 1911. It was sold when the Golf Club was re-sited in 1935. The hut then began a new life being re-sited to where it stood when I knew it. Ownership then passed to a Ned Fenwick and later again it transferred and this time to Duncan Morton, thus becoming known as Morton's cafe.

Ned Fenwick at the door, before it became Morton's Cafe.

In the 1950s, Morton's Cafe was run by Duncan Morton and his wife Lizzie, a pleasant lady with jet black hair tied in ringlets, I recall. Duncan only had one leg and had an artificial limb which was not of the quality as of today. I remember it gave out a loud creak followed by an equally loud thud each time he heaved himself about inside the shop. Duncan was a highly decorated war hero.

Duncan and Lizzie.

Duncan Edward Morton was 65 when he passed away in1981. His life story is a classic schoolboy's adventure from a fairground fighter to a war hero. From the age of 10, the Amble lad known as Duggie was a showman and boxer. At 14 he entered the ring as a professional under the name of Freddie Douglas.

During WW2 he became a sergeant in the Black Watch Regiment and lost a leg at Dunkirk. He was wounded 5 times and shell-shocked twice. He received several decorations including the Military Medal and 5 oak leaves.

After the war, he rejoined his father on the fairground circuit and started training boxers. Winters would be spent in Amble on the old fair site and in the summer they would tour between Yorkshire and Scotland.

Duncan at the rear, with 5 boxers and his Dad, far right.

Duncan settled in Amble in 1956 and opened a gift shop and general dealers i.e. the said Morton's Cafe but several years later had to retire because of ill health. He died before his wife leaving a daughter and grandchildren.

I only knew Duncan and his wife Lizzie as polite, courteous, hard-working shopkeepers. I only found his antecedents history during my research for this book. I am proud to have met them both.

Duncan was a fine, decent man and a true war hero. His life story is worthy of any film/documentary or book. His story could be straight out of a Catherine Cookson novel but with one significant difference, for his tale is true. Duncan Edward Morton, I salute you. RIP.

He and his wife lived in a wooden bungalow called Signal Cottage. It was on the cliff behind where the Seaview Cafe had been and overlooked Coquet Island, just off the coast of Amble. Without a doubt, it is a fantastic and much sought after position for a home. I believe new replacement apartments have been built on the site. Google maps only show a cleared area. Undoubtedly a primary reason for the recent planning permission being granted was the long term use of the site, as a residential property by the Morton family.

Duncan could often be seen on his, what must have been an immense struggle, daily trudge between his home and shop and in all weathers. My best memory of the shop was on each Saturday on sale were hot pies and mushy peas. Nothing was for consumption on the premises and was for take-away only. The customer would provide their own receptacle, usually a jug. It would be filled with the hot mushy peas and together with a pie, it proved to be a popular and substantial meal

Although a relatively small building, it must have been Tardis-like and well-stocked because the Morton's seemed to be able to produce, like a rabbit out of a hat, almost anything that was requested. The goods on offer included any not normally sold in small quantity. A 2lb bag of sugar could be divided and your half would be handed over in a paper bag. In the same way, a half-pound of Echo margarine, for example, would be divided and sold as a quarter pound. A pack of say, 10 Woodbines would I be equally split and the first 5 handed over in a paper bag. I learnt through my research that you could even buy one cigarette and a match. I do personally know that a pack of 5 Gillette razor blades was split and sold singularly.

A small packet of Brook Bond tea could also be split. I remember Brook Bond tea especially, because not only did it come with a card to collect a set, for instance, footballers etc. but importantly it also came with a Brook Bond stamp of value for collection. The stamp was on the outside of the packet and had perforations that had to be unpicked with a pin. The stamp would be then stuck onto a card, provided on request. The card held 60 stamps and when it was full you exchanged it in store for 5 shillings. (25p. in today's money but equivalent to £5.24p. in 1960.) So you will see that each stamp was worth one old penny.

Those Brook Bond stamps saw us Curry's and other families through some very tough financial times when my Dad was frequently off sick from the pit and we reverted to social security at such periods. My Mam's lifelong friend dear, Mrs Alice Ridgewell, still then residing in Newburgh St., with her lovely husband Tommy and family, shared those tough times and they supported each other throughout. I'd be sent with a message to Mrs Ridgewell saying, 'Have you got 5 or whatever, BB stamps to complete a card? Do you want the stamps refunded later or the 5 pennies?' If the stamps were available they'd be steamed off Mrs Ridgewell's card and stuck back onto my Mam's card. Then, the completed card would be taken to Morton's Cafe or elsewhere and the save the day 5 bob was obtained. Sometime later, Mam might get a similar request from Mrs Ridgewell.

Inside Morton's shop hung a sign which read, 'Please do not ask for credit as refusal can often offend.' Credit had been granted at one time but was terminated sometime later after Duncan had posted a list of names and addresses of his debtors outside the shop. The list was long and many hurried to see who was on it. Those who were in a position to, rushed to settle and thus have their name erased. I cannot remember if we were on the list but I would not be surprised if we were, such were the times.

I know that my Mam did run up debt at shops in Amble. I recall on occasions, being told to avoid going past so and so's shop, in case I was collared as to my Mam's whereabouts. It got so bad at one stage to get to school, I was setting off days earlier with sandwiches because I had to travel via Newcastle and double back to avoid all of them! (I do hope you are picking up on when I tend to exaggerate?)

Do you recall the meat slicing machines in shops at that time? Raw bacon would be sliced by winding a handle and you'd be asked to what thickness. Perhaps next it was the turn of corned beef and so on. The circular blade was only ever quickly wiped over with the same muslin cloth that lay next to the slicer. No one ever queried the health hazard and I cannot recall any illness caused (maybe not connected/proven) but that practice was best abandoned.

Here's a joke from back then. A feller got the sack from a wholesale meat supplier's because he was caught with his penis in the bacon slicer. The rumour spread and a mate enquired if there was any truth in the story? "Oh! Yes, it's quite true," he said. The enquirer asked, "Well, what a daft unhygienic and dangerous thing to do. What the hell did you do that for?" He said, "I don't know. A moment of madness I suppose but it wasn't entirely my fault. They sacked her as well."

DUNCAN MORTON'S PARENTS

Duncan's elderly parents were showground people and they had also settled in Amble. They lived just a few hundred yards south of Duncan's shop in Links Road, in an old travelling showman's caravan opposite, the entrance to Bobby Forsyth's farm, which is now the Granary bar/restaurant. As stated, old man Morton had at one time, had a boxing booth and toured the north with a fair.

Coincidently Duncan's Dad also only had one leg. Next to the caravan, they had what looked like a homemade small wooden roundabout for tiny tots with makeshift miniature cars fitted. Old man Morton would wind a handle thus propelling the antiquated contraption. I remember him whilst winding it at a snail's pace crying out, "Hold tight we're going to go fast." Anticipating that at any moment their precious darling would be subjected to G-force of great magnitude the concerned parent would point and also call out, "Hold on." These warnings I deduced only achieved one thing and that was to startle the poor unsuspecting child victim and most would end what should have been an enjoyable experience in tears.

I soon recognised the old man's call to be a clear indication that he was spent and the ride would be soon stopping. It seemed that the older he got the shorter the ride got. In the dying seconds, he would crank the handle so hard his arm would become but a blur. The kinetic energy transferred increased the pace from that of a snail to that of an elderly tortoise. I believe that instead of the obvious toll it took on him physically and the grindingly slow speed it produced, perhaps painted scenery being moved past the tots might have achieved precisely the same effect.

There were also 4 of what is colloquially known as a 'shuggy boat' in the northeast of England and is a fairground ride, in which pairs of riders pull ropes to swing back and forth. A similar ride called a pirate ship swings in a similar motion but without the rider pulling on a rope.

Mrs Morton with the shuggy boats and in the distance, Morton's Cafe.

Old Mrs Morton, for payment, would tell fortunes by card reading or she could do it with tea leaves if you preferred from inside her showman's caravan. Many of the womenfolk of Amble went to her, my Mam being one of them. For years Mam swore blind that the old woman could genuinely foretell the future. My two sisters went too and they wholeheartedly agreed with Mam. After a reading, they would relate every minute detail and in the 100% belief that it was genuine. I recall hearing stuff like, 'She said a man with fair hair would be marrying soon and would be happy.' Mam would say, "That's Joe he's marrying Bet." Mrs M might say, "I see a person in uniform overseas but don't worry they will be returning soon." Mam would say, "That's wor Alan and he's coming home on leave from Cyprus." Mrs M would say, "I see a man struggling with his health but don't fear he'll pull through." Mam would say, "That's Fred" and so it went on for years like that from the 3 of them, Mam Betty and Kath. I, a kid, had lots of feelings about it, fascinated, confused and I have to say it spooked me too. I asked, "Is Mrs Morton a witch?" I'd be told, "Don't be so daft of course, she's not a witch." I might say, "Well how can she tell what's going to happen if it hasn't happened yet?" I'd be told, "She's got a gift, that's how." I might say, "What gift, like a present do you mean. Does she make it happen?" Then it would end with a, "Yes a present. I'll tell you when you're older!"

Many years later as an adult, I started to wonder how Mrs Morton was able to hoodwink so many and for such a prolonged period. One thing I was 100% certain of, was she definitely could not see into the future. I racked my brains in search of everything I could remember hearing about the visits. Then it dawned on me and I'd finally solved the puzzle and it was so simple too. Now all this, 'A man with fair hair and a person in uniform overseas' and other mumbo jumbo stuff was to mislead/confuse and to appear to be a little hazy. Mrs Morton knew exactly who she was making the inferred references to. She could have come straight out with the information that Joe is going to marry Bet or Alan is coming home from Cyprus on leave from the army.

She was not going to give names because that would leave her wide open to suspicion by being too precise but how could she possibly know? She had been told. That's how. It is as simple as that, in a small pit village of less than 5000, where everyone knew everyone else. Yes, she could carry it off there but anywhere else bigger, no. She either would be stumped for something to say or the result would not have had the slightest hint of credibility and would have left her vulnerable to exposure.

 What helped me to discover her modus operandi, (method) was I recalled Mam and my two sisters saying on many occasions, what a lovely woman Mrs Morton was. After the reading, she didn't rush them away. She put the kettle on, she'd have a baked cake and she ALWAYS ASKED AFTER EVERYONE!

Of course, she did and perhaps all the responses were soon written down in a simple index system for future use. She would not have been able to shut Mam and my two sisters up, even if she'd wanted to. They loved to gossip. I can picture the scene now. Q. "Your neighbour is Mrs ? is her husband still in the forces?" R. "Yes, he's coming home on leave soon." Into the book, it would go for when Mrs ? arrived. Then, "I see someone in a
84

uniform due home soon." Afterwards, the kettle went on again and Mrs ? was asked, "Have you seen Mrs Curry and her two daughters? How are they getting on?" R. "They're fine. Betty's pregnant," etc. Right into the book, it would go. Mrs Morton would know exactly who her regulars were and would specifically guide the conversation around to them, during her after readings and all-important friendly chat.

Mrs Morton never foretold the future. She just told what she'd heard and packed it out with a helping of mumbo jumbo, intended to confuse and bewilder!

All fortune tellers have their own M. O. No fortune teller could tell you anything if as a total stranger you walked off the street and you told them absolutely nothing. They need the information to carry out the confidence trick.

MODERN DAY FORTUNE TELLER

Many years later, I was able to discover yet another modern-day M.O. of a fortune teller in Hastings. Someone I knew, Bob, told me that he'd had his fortune read by cards and how wonderful, this time a man, the teller was. They had never met before and Hastings has a population of about 100,000, 20 times more than that of Amble. So I knew that Mrs Morton's M.O. would not be possible in this case. I was not even sceptical on this occasion. I was positively a disbeliever but that seemed to encourage Bob to try and convince me the guy could genuinely foretell the future. The more I said it was baloney, the more Bob kept on and on. As far as I was concerned, I did not care much either way if he believed me or not but Bob was like a dog with a bone and would simply not let the matter go. He told me the guy has nothing to hide and he tape records every reading and the subject/victim is given a copy of the then cassette tape. Now I had to agree, this was novel and I said I'd be willing to listen to the tape if he wanted me to and this I did.

On hearing what was said, I agreed the detail given by the guy was quite amazing and certainly by far more than Mrs Morton was ever known to have given. Bob expected that finally I would be convinced by the tape and seemed to be declaring himself to be the winner, when I conceded that I was somewhat surprised by the content detail, considering there was no way he could have known Bob before the reading. I told Bob as convincing as it all may seem, the guy was undoubtedly a confidence trickster. Therefore he had to have some form of sophisticated M.O. Bob would have nothing of that, whatsoever.

You would have to know Bob to believe that he kept on about me being wrong and him right. So over many months when I saw him, mainly at a snooker club, we were both members of, the subject was brought up by Bob and we discussed it many times. Bob seemed to think because I could not be specific as to how the guy did it then he must be genuine, which of course was not the case. However, each time we spoke Bob gave more and more small details of the actual meeting culminating in me solving the puzzle.

A lot of people resort to consulting a fortune-teller because they are concerned about something and in Bob's case he was no exception. At the time of his reading, he was very depressed being in the throes of an acrimonious separation. He was driving people to despair with his, she said this and I wasn't going to put up with that etc. and that is what caused him to seek out a fortune-teller. I then started to think more about it and I quizzed him in minute detail as to what exactly took place, second by second and finally, I got to the bottom of it.

When Bob arrived at the address the guy's wife, who he also said was a lovely woman, said he was delayed on business but would not be long and would he mind waiting and she would put the kettle on. After a while, the guy turned up and the reading began immediately. So here we had a double act this time and you can bet your life our guy was delayed on business for every reading. The business he was delayed on was listening on an intercom to what 'the lovely wife' and the victim were chatting about. She would only have had to say, "Are you worried about something?" and she would have got the full nine yards! As for Bob, he just shrugged it off by saying, "You believe what you want and I'll believe what I want" and it was never mentioned again.

In my opinion, there should be no place in the 21st-century modern world for fortune-tellers, mediums or faith healers and they should be confined to history. They are nothing more than charlatans preying on the naive and vulnerable.

Here now is a topical story/joke. A guy who is a ventriloquist and cannot find work, in desperation seeks out an agent and enquires if he can find him any bookings. The agent said, "Sorry but it's old hat now. It's all been seen before, what with, Archie Andrews and

Peter Brough, Lennie the lion and Orville the duck etc. You just cannot get a booking nowadays for a ventriloquist act. I'll tell you what is popular now, mediums. I could get you a lot of work if you were a medium. Do you think you could be a medium?" The ventriloquist said, "It can't be that hard, sign me up because I need to do something." So he was signed up and the very next day, a woman contacted him via the agent. She said, "Are you a medium?" He said, "Yes." She said, "I have to contact my husband who passed away years ago. Can you do it?" He said, "Yes I can." She said, 'How much will it be?" He said, "It will depend on what you want really. There are 3 contacts I can do. For £20 you can get a message to him but he cannot reply." She said, "No, that one's no good I need a reply from him." He said, "Well the £50 contact should do you then and for that, you can speak to him and via me, he can reply to you." She said, "That one seems to be fine but what is the 3rd one?" He said, "That is what I call the extra special contact and for £100, you can speak to him and he can reply to you, again through me........whilst I'm drinking a pint of beer and smoking a cigarette." Within lies, a message and so beware!

THE RIDGEWELL FAMILY AND BOBBY THE MONKEY

I have mentioned that Mrs Alice Ridgewell was my Mam's lifelong friend. Mrs Ridgewell and her husband Tommy were a lovely genuine couple. They had 4 daughters and one son, John. It is safe to say that the Curry and Ridgewell families were in the same boat and helped each other when they could.

Linda, Sheila, Bobby the monkey and Mick.

In the 50/60s, they also acquired another addition to their family, that being Bobby the macaque monkey. John arrived home on leave from the merchant navy and had a friend in tow i.e. Bobby who was a real character and entertained us all with his antics. A monkey was a real novelty then and many had never seen one. Bobby lived in the lounge alongside the family. Bobby, of course, was the only monkey and at times he would crave female company and he looked for this from the cats. Mrs Ridgewell might suddenly jump up and shout at Bobby and shoo him away from a cat. Tommy used to say calmly, "Alice, don't do that if they have a litter we'll end up rich." Tommy might have been a firm advocate of 'desperate times call for desperate measures' and times were pretty desperate. No one knew if any such cross-relationship was ever consummated.

However, if you are in Amble and happen to see a cat peeling a banana, please let me know because I may know where it belongs!

John was a lovely guy just like his Dad but I don't think he ever knew about restrictions on the importation of animals. On a different occasion, when he returned on leave from being at sea, another friend accompanied him, a parrot. A well known Amblite, Lottie Stewart (Auntie Lottie) lived in Amble at that time. She was a fantastic lady and organised pantomimes every year, which were held in a local hall. So the story goes, Lottie, was putting on that year, Treasure Island with Long John Silver. She knew John had a parrot and so with the name John, at sea and with a parrot, he was an obvious choice for the lead part. He would be on shore leave at Christmas and was expected to be home.

It is said that John refused the part but now the reason gets a wee bit vague because of Amble folklore. You may realise what that can be like. You might also not be surprised to learn that I greatly contribute to it. Rumour has it, that because Lottie liked her stage productions to be as authentic as possible, John only turned down the part because she wanted him to have his leg off!

What happened next was John returned to sea and the parrot went on to have a very lucrative and successful acting career.

John and his wife, perhaps thinking of Bobby.

I saw this photo of the elephant on Amble beach. At first, I thought John has finally gone too far this time.

AMBLE HOSPITALITY

About 30 years ago, during one of my many back to my roots visits, which I require from time to time, for my Amble fix. I again stood briefly outside 47 Links Ave., as I recalled my living there and of my childhood. The lady occupant saw me and asked if she could help me. I told her that I had lived there and was reminiscing about those days. This lovely lady then asked if I'd like to look around the house, obviously knowing that would mean something to me.

Blimey, I was not going to miss that opportunity and with great appreciation, in I went. She guided me into every room including what had been my bedroom. How strange and in miniature, it felt. I have the same feeling anywhere I go in the town. It's because when I left, I was 2ft+ shorter than I am now. Hence for example the stone wall in Links Road, in the 50/60s, was maybe eye level and now I look down on it.

 The charming couple, never really knew how privileged I felt with their kind and unique gesture. It highlights Amble/NE impromptu hospitality at its very best. I didn't ask but how did she know what it would mean to me? Before leaving she took the time to update me on the Links Ave. residents then and gone. The lovely couple were Matty and Thelma Copeland. Sadly both have passed away now. I have been in touch with relatives who were unsurprisingly delighted to see the photo I had of the 3 of us at the front door and I am sure they will find my tale heart-warming.

Matty, Tom & Thelma.

CHAPTER 4

DARLINGTON

In 1963, I left my school friends and the town I loved and we moved to Darlington, not something my Dad or I wanted. It was purely my Mam's decision and we were never really consulted or given any choice in the matter. The reason for the move was simply because my Mam wanted to be near my eldest sister Betty, who had moved with her family and was living on the outskirts of Darlington.

There was no other reason to tear us away from our beloved Amble but my Dad complained little and was as usual compliant, albeit it was a wrench for us both. My Mam explained it away by saying there was a greater possibility of finding work for the two of them, there being many factories. It was said that my Dad who was in poor health, may find a little job sweeping up. Dad was not even capable of such a simple and mundane task on any permanent basis and no such job for either materialised. We merely struggled on with the help of social security.

It appeared that no consideration had been given to the fact that I was 14 and in my last year of schooling. It was obvious I would not be staying on for any further education and it was expected I would begin my working life without any academic qualifications whatsoever. I still find it hard to understand that being nearer to my married sister was worth the sacrifice of my schooling and the upheaval it caused to me to start a new school for about 1 year only, not forgetting the effect on my Dad.

My Dad had never seen the council house at Maidendale Cottages, which we were to occupy on the outskirts of Darlington. My Mam had arranged a council house swap with the previous occupants. When the removal lorry arrived my Dad and I could not believe what Mam had brought us to. To get there was via an un-adopted muddy pot-holed road. It was a terraced ex-railway cottage and had a bathroom but the toilet was once again at the end of the backyard. Mercifully this time, it was not a dry toilet as previously mentioned but a flush toilet. The people who got our Amble semi with inside toilet/bathroom must have been as delighted as we were downhearted. We settled in as best we could but my Mam was upbeat because Betty was only a short bus ride away.

FINAL SCHOOL YEAR

I started attending Darlington secondary modern boy's school part way through the final year. It was quite a long trek to and fro each day, much further than I was used to. It partly entailed me avoiding mud and potholes before reaching the made-up roads.

Shortly after we moved, Betty, her first husband and baby, Gordon, came to stay with us because they had lost their tied cottage. After a brief period, Betty and her family moved to Coventry. My Dad and I held our breath!

This was a very unhappy period in my life because although it was only about 70 miles from Amble, for a start my broad Geordie accent made me stand out from the rest and somewhat alienated me. Initially, I had no friends and I was bullied. I quickly found that Darlington had a different culture. Many were referred to as 'hawker boys,' being from a traveller's background and they talked of ponies and traps. Even at school they wore cravats and high laced heavy brown boots and were members of gangs.

One day a tiny youth dressed as described, hit me during a break in the schoolyard. It was entirely unprovoked and I made the mistake of retaliating but I was immediately set upon by a gang of 4 or 5 others. As I left school that same day, the gang set about me again. I was quite a tough kid and gamely fought back but I was easily subdued, outnumbered and overpowered by so many. So left battered and bruised I miserably trudged home. It was my first experience of how in Darlington scores were settled and so different from that of Amble. I had been involved in minor school scuffles in Amble but it was only ever on a one to one basis and only with fists.

I was now experiencing gangs attacking one solitary youth, whilst wearing boots and putting the boot in, which continued when the victim was on the ground. I had never experienced or witnessed this sort of fighting and it would never have been either actioned or condoned, by even a seasoned bully in Amble, of which there were very few. Clean fighting it seemed was not the order of the day in Darlington circles.

The day after my encounter, unsurprisingly depressed and not wanting to return to school battered and bruised, I did, not having made much of it to my parents. I decided to play it down and did
96

not report it to the school, mainly because I feared repercussions. There were a few nice kids in my class who accepted me and eventually I was left alone. I was fully aware from then on, without provocation, what to expect if I or anyone else became targeted. Later, I found my own experience of bullying gave me a greater understanding of how a kid felt if he/she were to experience the cruelty and misery it can cause.

DAD DIES

Dad's marriage to Mam continued to be unhappy. He struggled with his health, not too many years after the war. He'd worked hard when his health allowed both on the farms and then in coal mining. He knew none of the good things in life, like a nice, home and car or what it was like to live without money worries. I don't think he ever went to a restaurant for a meal. Dad was in a bad way by now and his mind started to wander too. Eventually, he was bedridden and Mam did everything for him.

After a few months, Dad was taken to hospital and died two days later on 28 July 1965 of a cerebral haemorrhage, he was 58. I was 15 and 8 months and now alone with my widowed Mam.

I was deeply saddened when my Dad passed away. He had not had much of a life and apart from the war, he had not been anywhere outside of the UK. He'd never had a holiday, except going to my sister Betty's when she lived briefly in Scotland. He was not a drinker and if he had a few Woodbines, he only smoked a couple per day and a football newspaper called a pink, he seemed happy. He liked nothing better than, as my Uncle Joe did, walking the Amble beaches on a lovely day with me or with our dog.

The photos of him where he looks about 70, were taken when he was just in his 40s, break my heart. He was a thoroughly good and decent man. What a shame that later in life, when I could do something to make his life more bearable, he is no longer with us.

A MOVE TO FIRTHMOOR ESTATE

Mam and I moved from the ramshackle ex-railway cottage a few thousand yards to a more modern council house on a close-by estate. At least now we no longer had to negotiate the unmade road. The new to us place was no palace but importantly we were back living in a house with an inside toilet again.

Not long after we moved, there was a total breakdown in Betty's marriage and she returned to live with us again but in addition to tiny tot Gordon, there was now a new baby girl, Julie. Betty was not with us long before she got re-housed to a council house, over the road from us. We were all happy with that arrangement.

I START WORK

It was a very happy day indeed when at the age of 15 I left school without any qualifications whatsoever and I could not get out the gates quick enough. It may have been a different feeling had I continued at Amble but I believe the outcome would have been the same, at 15 I would have left.

As coal mining was coming to its end and with the lack of a job opportunity, had I remained in Amble I may have found myself, as had been predicted so many times, on the dole along with many of my school friends but I was in Darlington and I have to say there was more job scope for me.

A week after I left school, I started with J. L. Moore's wholesale fruit and vegetable suppliers sited, below the Darlington covered market in the town centre. My job was to hump, fetch and carry the produce, including supplying the market upstairs. How I struggled with heavy potato sacks in particular. I started at 6 am and I was told there was no set finishing time, only when the day's work was completed. The first week I was there the elderly director who also worked in the warehouse, would hand me for example, an apple followed by a pear, then grapes and this went on each day. I found out later that there was a method behind his appeared madness. He was endeavouring to sicken me of fruit and thus I would have little interest in it for my personal use long term. All the workers did receive a large bag of assorted fruit and vegetables every Friday. My Mam thought this to be a huge treat but it proved to be a one-off occurrence.

One day during the first week, at about 6 pm, I was preparing to go home but I was told I had to go to Darlington railway goods yard with a lorry driver, to take delivery of bananas that had just arrived. Due to the late hour, I was not much pleased but off I went. The bananas were transported in a box van and were in heavy bunches. They were wrapped in brown paper and polythene. They had to be unloaded from the rail box van onto the lorry and transported back to the warehouse, where they were unloaded again. The coverings were then stripped away and the bananas were taken into the warehouse and hung in a windowless room with a naked gas flame and left to ripen. I was told to look out for spiders and scorpions. By the time the work was done it was after 8 pm.

About the middle of the second week after a few 6 pm finishes, I was preparing for home and I was once again, without any prior warning, told that I had to do another banana run. I was again not pleased but reluctantly I completed the task as before. The previous week, I cannot remember how much my take-home wage was but it was less than £5. I considered this was not acceptable, due to the long and unpredictable hours and hard work expected of a mere boy of 15. I voiced my opinion and was told that if I did not like it I had to go. I got my coat and go I did. I had lasted 2 weeks.

My Mam was not amused I can tell you. I can remember her saying, "What the hell is going to become of you, two weeks and you've got the sack!" I corrected her by saying that I had not exactly got the sack and that I had resigned. That only made her madder and to be fair it must have been disconcerting, to say the least.

Mam had not moved with the times and often seemed to think in the same subservient way, as in the days she referred to when she was in service on the farms, when lowly farmhands had to do as they were told, accepted low wages and worked long hours, under threat of losing not only their job but also their tied cottage.

A week later, I started work at a factory in Darlington called Amdega. My take-home pay was a paltry, £2. 8s. 4d per week. It was an engineering factory and the work was tedious.

After a few months I was still at Amdega, split into three two letters, it stood for ambition, determination and gain. I saw little or no gain so with my ambition and determination and in further pursuit of better gain, giving notice, I moved on. Once again, Mam was not pleased.

DARLINGTON BR

One of the few friends I made was working at Darlington British Rail, at Bank Top mainline station. On a whim, I called at the station master's office and enquired about any job prospects. Almost immediately, I was given a written test and then personally interviewed on a one to one basis, by the station master, Mr Renton, in his private office with a roaring coal fire. He at all times, including when in his office, wore a black bowler hat, black jacket, pinstripe trousers, white shirt and grey-black spotted tie. He was a big man, overweight but very smartly turned out. He wore half lens spectacles and peered over the top of them, in a schoolmasterly way, as he spoke to me, gently, slowly and with a very broad Scots accent. He verbally tested me on simple spelling and general knowledge, which I answered with ease.

After a short while, Mr Renton being satisfied said that he was happy to offer me employment as a lad porter. This was a title for an employee under 18 years of age and involved no porter duties as such. The wage was more than I had been getting and so I started straight away.

So here I was, at the very hub of British Rail, at the bustling Darlington mainline station and where it all began in 1825, with George Stephenson's, 'The Locomotion No. 1,' which first ran between Darlington and Stockton and stood on display on the platform at Darlington Station, from 1892 until 1975. It was re-housed to The Head of Steam Museum, Darlington. To think, I passed that piece of British railway history every working day, whilst employed at the station. I get goose-bumps just thinking about being a small part of it.

I was now at a happy time in my employment life. I was excited, as I thought any young man would be, being around steam engines and getting paid seemed to be a bonus. The sight of a steam engine being fired up and the smell of steam on metal still thrills me to this day. I was fully aware that right at that moment, I was living through a piece of rail steam history but the end was nigh. I knew it was the beginning of the end for the steam engine and it was fast becoming the new era of the diesel.

My first duty was as a messenger boy to the goods yardmaster. I had to carry paperwork between the station master's office and the various goods yards dotted around Darlington. Frequently I walked and crossed the busy mainline between York and Newcastle, often negotiating the track at a safe time, as the Flying Scotsman shot past, with the golden thistle and side wings emblazoned on the front above the diesel cab. The more famous steam version had already been retired in 1963.

A big part of my duty was to visit the homes of goods guards, to either call them out or with a change of shift. Very few had telephones back then. I was given bus tokens to use on the local bus but was told if I chose to walk, I could keep them for my own use. I had a maroon Vespa scooter by then. I rode it without a crash helmet and at breakneck speed. I had many falls from that machine but still had no fear. So I could walk or ride and still build up a store of tokens, which my Mam thought were very handy.

I was then moved to another goods yard on the outskirts of Darlington on the way to Croft and my main duties changed. As the engines entered the goods yard I had to count the wagons in and out and enter the details on a daily traffic sheet. I had to then call the signal box as and when the trains left the yard. The internal phones were all Morse code type tap phones and each had a different code, e.g. dot, dot, dash etc. but you soon learnt to ignore the codes that sounded all the time, unless it was yours of course.

I was told that my priority job was to make sure the huge kettle was filled and kept boiling at all times on the gas ring. The reason being, on entering the yard the fireman would hop off the engine, be it steam or diesel, with his swing handle white enamel billycan, to seek hot water for tea. I was told that nothing takes priority over that boiling kettle, including phones and counting wagons. If wagons were missed the numbers could be retrieved later from the yard shunters or if it was a departing engine, you could phone and ask a signalman to supply the count. That was how it was to be, throughout my time in that job.

At that time on the railway, your duty times were very odd. For instance, the early shift was from 6.18 am to 1.37 pm and I never knew why and no one else appeared to or for that matter care either. My late shift was 1.37 pm to 9.18 pm but I never worked past about 6.30 pm. The reason being that another important job I had was to go to the off licence when it opened at 6 pm and fetch the beers for the late shift shunters and yard inspector. I was then relieved of my duties and allowed to go home and my duties were covered by those remaining. If the off licence had opened earlier or there had been supermarkets then, I guess my day would have finished even earlier. No one ever had more than a pint or two but it was strictly forbidden nevertheless.

After about a year, I had a call to attend the station master's office, a place I visited frequently on errands but I had never been called there and so with some trepidation, I presented myself. I was told Mr Renton wants to see you. Anxiously, I entered his office and with the normal coal fire roaring, there he sat with his bowler hat on, as usual. I was quickly put at my ease and a smiling Mr Renton said, "The lad in oor office is 18 the noo and its time for him to move on cos he wants to be a guard. I would like ya ta tak his place, de a wanna dee it?" I said, "Thank you Mr Renton, I would." He smiled and said, "Yer a gud lad Tam and we'll look after ye if you carry on as yer deein, away an see Dennis tha noo an he'll arrange everythin wi ye." With that, I departed and went next door to see the head clerk, Dennis and I was given the details of my new remit. I knew this was a great opportunity as anyone completing his time in the post, on reaching 18, had to move on. What they moved on to, seemed to be from past history, any job

104

of their choice, within reason but would cover most, such as driver, signalman or in my predecessor's case, a guard.

A few days later, I took up my new duties and became the lad porter in the station masters office, a plum job at my level and the envy of all the other lads and you will soon see why. I would work from 8.30 am to 5.30 pm Monday to Friday. However, I would be paid 50% more, as a goodwill gesture but in return, I would be expected to be trusted with confidentialities. I would also give and take on the odd occasion if I was required to work late but I never was. I realised immediately it was a huge increase in wages for little in return and I was delighted of course. The only other condition was that my deal was to be kept strictly secret from all. My agreement was but a formality.

So an even happier time opened up for me in my new appointment. I kept my head down and did everything that was required of me. I delivered paperwork to signal boxes and goods yards, simple office duties such as running off copies on the Roneo ink printing machine. There were no digital printers back then. The Roneo was the state of the art machine to have. The typist typed the script onto a waxed-paper stencil referred to as a 'skin', which wrapped around a roller drum and after injecting the ink you manually turned a handle, one revolution produced one ink copy. Too much ink or a tear and it easily spoiled, meaning with great apologies the typist repeated her process and you began again. It was tedious and at best messy.

I got into the office half an hour before everyone else and opened up. After collecting the mail and opening it, that was it until 9 am when the typists and clerks arrived, including chief clerk, Dennis, who was very efficient but still had time to be amiable and enjoy a joke. There were 4 clerks and 2 typists. There was always stuff for me to do but I was not overloaded. I got on with everyone and there was not once that I had to be disciplined and I seemed well-liked both inside the office and by the many outside too.

Many times, I was privy to information that was treated with secrecy but I kept my word and it remained so, as far as I was concerned. In my privileged position, those outside the office, the hundreds of drivers, guards, ticket collectors, porters, shunters, maintenance, cleaners, not forgetting the British Rail Transport Police and all the others, that keep a main-line station running smoothly, all knew me and where I worked. With this in mind, there were many times, that I was asked about certain internal station master matters but my lips were sealed. I simply replied by saying, "They don't discuss things in front of me" or simply by saying, "I don't know." Everyone outside the office seemed to make a special effort to engage me in conversation and befriend me.

I still had to take letters, documents and train timetables to the outlying signal boxes only, no goods yards. I had the choice of walking, using the bus with tokens or my scooter. No one seemed to care which method I used or how long it took, only that it was done. As everyone appeared to be my friend, I hit on another most enjoyable form of transporting myself and the post. I would leave the station crossing the mainline to the goods yard. From there I would hop on the footplate of the next available steam goods train and if I wanted to get off at a certain signal box, I would call upon the driver to slow the train allowing me to alight and once I had visited the box I could use the same method to return. Sometimes, it was not possible but most times it was but if I was in a hurry I might have to settle for a diesel engine.

The mainline at Darlington BR station, in the 60s, at the point where I crossed almost daily.

As a kid, I never had what others took for granted, for example, I would have loved a train set. However, things were looking up now. I had a steady job which allowed me to obtain a motorised Vespa scooter, albeit second-hand which I was paying for on HP. I promised myself that I would honour, without fail, the HP agreement and remembering my Mam's quote in fending off court actions, even if I had to find a way to 'get blood out of a stone.'

Uniquely, I was now in a privileged position to be manipulating and playing with the biggest train set one could ever imagine being possible. Here I was right at the very heart of and in the birthplace of railway transport itself. I realised now that train sets were for kids. I no longer cared that I never did have one. As the saying goes 'all things come to those who wait', finally my patience was being rewarded because now I had the real thing and I was living every train enthusiast's dream.

A big event every Friday, which I took a part in, stands out in my memory and that was payday. Soon after 9 am, Dennis and I would leave the office, taking with us a very large brown canvass two-handled holdall. We then met a cash security van at the front entrance gates to platform 1. The bag was handed to a guard who passed it to another, inside the rear of the van. After a time, the now heavy bag was handed back to us. With Dennis holding one handle and me holding the other, we then walked as casually as we could, along the platform and returned to the office.

Half a dozen clerks were then locked inside an upstairs room and busied themselves with making up the wage packets. Later that same day, the wages would be collected via a small window by the employees. I did see the contents of the bag on many occasions and although I never knew exactly how much cash it contained. I do know it was several thousands of pounds. When I look back now I realise only too well, how vulnerable we were from attack and being robbed of that substantial amount of cash. I am surprised that such a regular collection was not spotted and targeted.

I was sent on a 2-week initial junior management course at Stockton and I was the youngest there. I was told that it would give me an understanding of the greater workings of the managerial side of British Rail. I will never know if there was more in store in that direction. The course went without a hitch and then I returned to my normal daily tasks and for the time being, I was content with my lot.

THE MALLARD

I recall having a rail story related to me, which caused me to envy the second husband of my sister Betty, Mick Kirtley. Mick had been a fireman based at Darlington. It would have been sometime in the early 1960s when he was the standby fireman at Darlington. He was whiling away the time playing cards when he was told that he had a job. He groaned but then he was told he was wanted for The Mallard. The blue beauty still holds the steam engine speed record of 126 mph on 3 July 1938, which remains unbroken to this day. It is now unlikely ever to be broken. Mick thought at first it was a wind-up because The Mallard did not stop at Darlington. So how could it be, that he was required? Well, it was true and Mick would fire it up as far as its next official stop, Newcastle. The reason being the regular fireman had been taken ill. What a unique privilege.

My eldest brother Alan at that time was living in Worthing Sussex. He convinced me that there were much better work opportunities in the south of England. Even though British Rail was considered reasonably secure, he felt I could achieve better. He advised that I should move away from the environment in Darlington. In other words, my family life was lacking and my Mam's world seemed to revolve, as it always had, around Betty and to a lesser extent my sister Kath and the grandkids. I knew for sure that the strong bond between Mam and my sisters, especially Betty, would continue and that she would be perfectly happy. Alan said that I could lodge with him, his wife and his baby son, David until I was settled. I decided he was right and I said that I would take him up on his offer.

It will be apparent by now, of the deep affection, which I still have, for steam trains and all things connected but what may not be so clear is how I could turn my back on that for the unknown. I grapple with the answer to that myself but what I do know is that I desired more than my parents ever had. I did not have any urge to be rich but I did want what normal people had and not to feel like a second class citizen anymore because if you are on the bottom rung of the social scale, that is what you feel like.

With the offered support of my brother, it might just be the kick-start I needed. Alan had convinced me that British Rail was not going to transport me much further on my life's journey and I was now keen to take the first step. Even though this was one of the happiest periods of my working life, I would ultimately decide to take myself off, moving south to Worthing Sussex. I'd be leaving my widowed Mam in Darlington but I was convinced she was happy enough with my sister Betty living just across the road. My other sister Kath also lived not far away in Darlington with her husband John and her son Alan.

So in 1966, I told my Mam I intended to leave my British Rail job and head south. As anticipated, she thought resigning from a good job on the railway was stupid. Eventually, she came to accept that I had made my mind up and she said she hoped it would work out well for me but she thought it likely, that I would return.

As for the reaction from the station master's office, they were all shocked and said they did not want to lose me. Mr Renton seemed genuinely disappointed but he along with the others wished me good luck. He added that if it did not work out as I hoped, as long as he was in charge there would be a job for me if I returned at any time. This was a very generous offer and of course, lessened my risk. He provided me with a 'To whom it may concern,' glowing reference.

Another extra concession I had been granted, was although rail workers were allowed, I think, 4 privilege anywhere tickets per year, I was told no record of my quota would be kept and therefore I could have as many as I wanted. I never abused this. I only recall having 2 or 3 at the most, during the approximate 18-month duration of my employment. Dennis asked how I was travelling to Sussex and I said it would be by rail, of course, adding jokingly, "I know all the drivers, Dennis." He was fully aware of my footplate hopping. Without any further ado, he issued me with a single open ticket to Worthing Sussex saying, "If you decide to come back anytime, let me know and I'll send you a ticket." Even now, I still find this gesture genuinely touching.

Sadly, I never saw or heard of those kindly folk again. I do regret not making the effort to revisit them. My consolation is that all obligations were fully served on both sides during a very pleasant period. I was going to miss playing with my train set but it was time to venture forth and maybe I would find replacement toys.

DO YOU WANT TO HEAR A BANG NANA?

Before moving on, I want to relate a story that took place in the house occupied by Betty involving my Mam and Gordon. As I said, Betty's home was just over the road from my Mam which suited them both down to the ground. Betty had married her second husband, after a bad experience with her first. She had been a single mother since the two kids were very young and had struggled to bring them up. She still occupied a council house as my Mam did but she had finally found a husband who was a good worker and for once in her life, she could rely on a regular weekly wage coming in.

So for the first time in her adult life, she was able to obtain a brand new suite and a fitted carpet. The said items were obtained on HP and were not what you would term as being of quality but to Betty, they were the best. One day, Betty was out shopping and had taken Julie with her. Mick was at work and the early teens Gordon was at home. He had acquired a moped and was tinkering with it in the rear garden. My Mam thought she would take advantage of the peace, quiet and comfort of Betty's new items. So she settled in front of the open coal fire, seated on the new sofa and began to read the newspaper. Mam was easily pleased and must have felt reasonably content because she liked to read the paper and so all was peaceful and quiet.

112

After a short while, Gordon came in and said, "Do you want to hear a bang, Nana?" Engrossed in the paper, Nana said casually and without looking up, "Aye if you like." Suddenly there was a terrific bang and burning coals from the fire were blasted out into the room, some hitting Nana and causing the newspaper to catch fire. The startled Nana leapt to her elderly feet and stamped out the burning paper, whilst screaming at Gordon, who had taken flight, "Laddie, I'll murder you." He had thrown a bulb from the moped onto the fire and of course, it exploded but with much more force than anyone could have imagined. Although the singed Nana was unhurt, the worst part was the cushions of the new sofa were burnt and also the new fitted carpet, just in front of the fire. Gordon was still missing when Betty returned and only having made a few payments on the new items, they were now quite severely damaged and even worse uninsured.

Gordon had been circulated as being wanted and much later he sheepishly returned, to face the music with his Mam and just before Mick was due home. After many apologies, his Mam decided to forgive him, just as all mothers do. A plan was hatched, so Mick would remain blissfully unaware of the earlier incident. A rug was placed over the burnt carpet in front of the fire, the sofa cushions were turned over and a loose cover placed over it, thus disguising the damage to both. Mick was told the rug looked cosier and the sofa was covered to protect it.

It was ages before he discovered the damage and Betty told him there must have been a detonator amongst the coals and she continued to hide the true facts from him. It was years later when

Mick was told the truth and by that time the heat had died down in more ways than one! Although not so funny at the time, my family have laughed about it since. Gordon remains full of devilment to this day, albeit now in his fifties. Thankfully there have been no further bangs!

CHAPTER 5

SUSSEX

Soon came the day when I boarded the southbound train and full of hope I headed for Worthing. I was welcomed by both Alan and Sylvia his wife, into their home. They looked after me extremely well. I enjoyed the new order in my life that accompanied the organised way Sylvia ran a home. She had been a nurse and Alan had been in the army and so everything was almost regimented and I found I liked that very much indeed. I fitted in well and there was never any disagreement. My nephew David was only about one year old but he was very well behaved.

Alan worked for Birds Eye Frozen foods as an HGV delivery driver and occasionally relief manager at the Lancing depot. His lifetime all-consuming passion was flying and every weekend he was to be found at the Southdown Gliding Club, at Firle Beacon Alfriston. It became accepted that at any social get together, such as christenings, weddings, birthdays etc., if it took place at weekends, Alan was conspicuous by his absence but he would make an exception for a funeral. Friday evening Alan would arrive home from work and then soon after he would be off gliding until he returned Sunday evening. He would bunk at the clubhouse ready for the following morning as soon as it was daylight.

Most times he would have Sheba his golden Labrador with him. She was so gentle with everyone, especially David. Her only annoying habit was, if there were any cowpats she would roll in them and be completely covered. I am told it is not uncommon to find this with that breed. Sheba found plenty of cowpats on the airfield at the top of the beacon, for the field was occupied by cows and sheep. Gliders seemed to just take off and land whilst negotiating a way around them. The sheep ran away but the cows just stood and looked. The club was not a money-making concern and was run by the members. It appeared to me that 90% of Alan's time was spent either operating the winch tow line, manually pulling gliders about or just talking flying and the remaining 10% was in the air. Alan thought I might be interested in the gliding. I went up once in the two-seater and thought it to be ok as a one-off but it was not going to hold my attention, as the 10% in the air did not seem to compensate for the 90% groundwork. So I decided that any toys replacing my beloved steam engines would be firmly on the ground and not in the air.

Alan may have been disappointed that I did not want to join the gliding club because he would have had someone at home to talk flying with, which he could not get enough of. He never really got excited about anything else and I thought Sylvia was an absolute gem to go along with it. They had a lovely tidy home which they were buying and a newish Hillman Minx car and a half share in a high performance sleek white glider and tow trailer. All the things I hoped I would have one day, except for the glider and trailer. They were not well off but they were certainly living better than I had been used to and of course that applied to Alan when he was young and at home too.

Sylvia was so frugal with money and a great budgeter but a nightmare to go food shopping with, which I tried to avoid after a couple of experiences. Where they lived was a bus ride away from the town centre but she walked everywhere and with David always in tow. There were no supermarkets then and so for example, she would go into the butchers and price the sausages and then to another butcher to compare the price. No, the first one was the cheapest by 3 pennies and so it was back to the first one again. We saved maybe 2 bob and shoe leather used was a pound, I reckon.

Before buying anything major, she would always consult Alan but he did not want to know really. As far as he was concerned he had every confidence in Sylvia and it was of little importance to him and he would often answer with indifference. I recall one such occasion when she said to him, "Alan can I have a new pair of boots?" I suddenly thought he might check her old ones as mine had been, by the social security visiting officer and if he was satisfied he'd issue her with a voucher. Just to be awkward and not because he meant it, he replied without looking up from the newspaper, "No." Sylvia said, "Alan and why can I not have a new pair of boots when you have a glider?" Once again without looking up he said, "It's simple because you can't fly boots!" Sylvia was not generally known as a wit, came right back at him saying,

"What about if we compromise and settle on a pair of flying boots then?" Alan maybe not wishing to accept he'd been had, stayed hidden behind the paper and said, "The answer is still, no." Sylvia and I laughed. Although he never would deprive his family of anything they needed, I often wondered if that was how Alan viewed life because his priority was always flying first and everything else came second.

I settled into the routine in the Alan and Sylvia household and the next important task was to find new employment. I went to the Worthing dole office and they told me there might be a job available at a small factory, a few hundred yards down the road from Alan and Sylvia's house. I thought that was handy because I'd left my scooter in Darlington. So I went for an interview. The money was poor, less than £4 a week and I told the interviewing manager so. He said that if I took the job after 2 weeks if he thought I was ok, he would consider an increase. So I started and the job was standing at a drill all day, drilling small pieces of brass. Others were doing the same job and some were on lathes. A buzzer sounded for all breaks. It was brain-numbingly tedious and not even well paid. I stuck to it and I thought I'd given good value during the 2 weeks. I spoke again to the manager and reminded him of what he'd promised. He responded by saying that he didn't know me yet and I'd have to give it longer. I thought if he wanted to get to know me he was about to miss his chance and with that, I resigned. I had saved a little bit and I thought I can pay my very low dig money.

SHOREHAM CONCRETE FACTORY

Alan said he agreed with my decision and just to try elsewhere. I checked the Brighton Argus newspaper and found young lads were wanted at a factory in Shoreham, 8 miles away. I thought I better get my scooter sent down and I arranged for a friend to collect it from my Mam's and to have it sent by rail to Worthing. It arrived undamaged and I started riding it again. I had an interview at the Shoreham factory and was accepted. This time the money was good, at £10 a week. The factory manufactured concrete spacers, which are pieces of concrete of different size and shape, for example, a horseshoe shape. The spacer fits into a mould at the centre to hold metal strengthening bars in place, whilst concrete is poured in, to make for instance concrete posts or lamp posts etc. There are many other uses but there is little point in getting bogged down with unnecessary detail.

To give a rough guide as to the job, I stood at a bench and a wet cement mix was shovelled onto the bench. I had a rough glove on my right hand and a thin washing up glove on my left. A metal mould, no bigger than a saucer with a handle, was fitted to the bench and inside the mould could be a variety of different shapes. I grabbed a handful of cement with the right-hand rough glove and slapped it into the mould. I tapped it firm with a stick with my left hand and then another handful of cement went onto the top of it and I then smoothed it off with the right hand. I then pushed the handle up and the cement was then raised above the mould. Carefully with my left hand and very gingerly at first, I picked it up and placed it on a tray to dry. Then I repeated the action all day.
118

At first, you break many picking them up but after a while, you get the hang of it and you can do it without thinking.

There were about 20 of us there all about the same age. There were bonuses to be had when you got fast. Surprisingly, the day did not drag and it was a jovial and pleasant atmosphere, mainly because a pop radio went all day and there were no problems about us talking, cracking jokes and laughing, which of course suited me down to the ground. The work continued and the manager and boss were very nice. We did a change around and each of us got to do the mix for a day and that made a change from doing the mould work.

I was still paying off my scooter and had paid about 75% before leaving Darlington. The payments were 10 shillings a week (50p.) That does not sound much but it was a 1/8th of my wage if I'd stayed at the previous place but only 1/20th at the new one and that was good. Every Saturday, I went to the post office and got a postal order for 10 shillings. I posted it with a return s.a.e and enclosed my re-payment card. The motorcycle shop endorsed my card and posted it back to me.

For cash, I bought a made to measure suit, not with two pairs of trousers. I was not going to be taking any shortcuts under barbed-wire fences, whilst wearing this one. I also got some other new clothes and a watch from Sylvia's catalogue club and paid weekly for them as well as my digs. The home was run like a well-oiled machine. My clothes were washed and ironed to perfection. The bed got changed at regular intervals on the same day of the week. I knew what was on the menu every mealtime and that suited me down to the ground. I loved the organised way Sylvia ran the home, a thing I'd never had but craved. After paying my way, I still could save, something I'd always done, no matter how little it might be. I liked the security it gave to know I had a nest egg.

One morning on the way to work, a car pulled out in front of me and I hit it. I fell from the scooter and broke my collar bone. The bike was a write-off. The police reported the other driver for driving without due care and attention and he was prosecuted. He pleaded not guilty. I went to Steyning Court and gave evidence. He was found guilty and fined which undoubtedly helped my insurance claim. I was paid out but it was not a great amount. I paid the scooter off and I felt proud that I'd never missed any payment. I was 17 and I felt considering how things had been, I had achieved something.

I had applied for my motorcycle test before the accident and I got a date but now I had no scooter. My brother Ray had moved out of his digs in Worthing and was now married and living in Woodingdean, Brighton. Ray had a Cento scooter and so I borrowed that for the test. On the day the exhaust kept coming apart and I had to get off now and again and kick it back on. I took the test in Worthing and I did not know the streets. With a motorcycle test, the examiner tests you on foot. Him on foot, not you! He gives the candidate directions where to go and he walks around the streets watching you but you don't know where he is half the time. Anyway, what with the scooter being new to me, the exhaust loose and not knowing the area, I got lost and I was away ages. We eventually stumbled across each other again. He said, "Where have you been?" I told him I'd got lost and he asked me some Highway Code questions. I passed first go and I was self-taught.

After my collar bone had healed I was back at work but now I was travelling via Southern Rail from East Worthing Halt to Shoreham every day. The difference was this time I was not travelling on the footplate of my beloved steam engines but in a carriage of a diesel engine and much worse I was a fare-paying passenger. Not only that I thought, but I had now lost my toys, no scooter and no train set. Time to think about getting some replacements and so having gone off bikes somewhat, I decided to start having car driving lessons. The scooter had given me road awareness and so I thought I might not need many. At £1 an hour, I thought that is not cheap!

Back at the factory, it was not at all tedious and it was quite enjoyable. I got to be fast and probably could do it blindfolded and still earn some weekly bonus but it was a dead-end job. I hadn't left British Rail to come to Sussex for this, so I began to think about moving on once again but to what?

Most of the lads at the factory seemed to be not very bright and maybe would be stuck doing that type of work for the rest of their lives but I knew I was not cut out to be a manual worker permanently.

One of the lads there was touching stuff with 'DANGER' written on it. When it was his turn to look after the canteen room, everyone complimented him on how their mug had gone from dark brown to gleaming white with one wash. Then we found out he'd used Harpic toilet cleaner on them! It turned out he was trying to conceal the fact that he could not read or write. He was a nice lad and I took it upon myself to try and teach him to read during tea and lunch breaks. I took one of my nephew's books in and sat in a corner with him and after a very short while I felt we might be getting somewhere. The other guys played cards during our breaks and moaned from time to time at us saying for example, "Is it not time to have a change from the Big Bad Wolf and the 3 Little Pigs?"

There was also another quite withdrawn lad there by the name of Richard Bari Tuck, known as Bari. I felt sorry for him because he was small and skinny and quite pathetic but because I made an effort to be friendly, he seemed appreciative. I recall that I spent a few days on a one to one basis with him because we were allowed outside to sit in the sunshine, whilst we attached metal springs to a big batch of plastic spacers. We got on fine but I'm not being unkind when I say we were not on the same wavelength. You will hear more about Bari later.

CHAPTER 6

WEST SUSSEX CONSTABULARY POLICE CADETS

One day when I was checking the job adverts in the newspaper again, I saw one for prospective police cadets for the West Sussex Constabulary. I had never considered being a policeman mainly because maybe I thought it was above my capabilities. Alan said to me, "Anything in there?" I said, "Nowt really, only an advurt fur polis cadets." Now do not overlook the fact that is how I spoke. Alan asked if I fancied that and I said I did but I thought you had to be bright to be a 'polis'. Alan said I should not be so daft and he thought I could do it. "Just apply. What have you got to lose?" he said. So I did but if Alan had not given me the support and encouragement, I would not have gone ahead.

I received a letter back requesting me to attend Oakland's House at Chichester for a morning of exams followed by an interview in the afternoon. I told the manager at the factory and the day off was booked and all wished me good luck.

On the morning, there were 2 girls and 14 lads including me, all hoping to join. An Inspector Eric Hollin was in charge that day. I sat the exams and I was pretty confident with spelling and dictation. I was quite good in that regard but I never did study, for anything, it just happened. There was a general knowledge paper and I thought that was a cinch. The maths was the problem. I remember there was a 'pi equals to' question. I thought what the hell is that all about?

We didn't even do that at my basic pit village school. I thought pi must be equals to 3 or 4 sausage rolls or 2 pasties at least. I remember once being told, something like, 'Always take pi to 2 decimal places' but I must have misheard and whenever I went to Birmingham and West Bromwich, I took a pork pie with me because I thought I'd been told, 'Always take pie to two dismal places.'

I was never interested in maths at school because it was all 'Tommy has 6 apples and if he eats 2' etc. When I left school, I started to understand it better because when it came to pound notes I got more interested instead of apples. I truly believe my real education started after and not during my schooling. Anyway, I did what I could on the maths paper and I could do no more.

Then it was lunchtime and some of the candidates went off saying they were going to a so and so restaurant. They all sounded posh to me at that stage and so I went off on my own. Even though I was not 18 yet, I went to a pub and I think I had two pints. That did not affect me whatsoever because I had started drinking and going to pubs at 16 up north.

Come the afternoon we were interviewed individually. We the candidates waited together in one room and were called in one by one and then those having been interviewed came out and rejoined the waiting group. I remember the group asked each other in turn what qualifications each person had gained. Every person said something like, "I've got 5 GCE's" and so on. When it came to me I said, "Wey a haven't got any like. A left school when a was 15 an av bin wurkin." So after that, I reckoned if this were a horse race I would be the rank outsider, for sure. It came to my turn and I was not worried at all. I'd had a few interviews and knockbacks were not new to me and I'd handled disappointment before.

There were two or maybe three interviewers present including Inspector Hollin. They asked me questions and I can remember one started to speak before I'd answered the other's question. I politely said that I would answer the other one first. It's only a guess but I think that was a pre-planned ploy to unnerve. They mentioned my glowing British Rail reference and my teacher's. They also referenced the maths paper and I reminded them of my basic education. Inspector Hollin said something like, "We like your English paper results and in the police that is the important one. Your maths is not that bad that you couldn't work out the mileage you'd done in a police car." Inspector Hollin told me his wife was from the NE and he knew the area. That was easy, I thought and out I went to rejoin the rest again.

Eventually, everyone had been seen and we were told to wait to be called in again individually to be informed if we had been successful or not. Everyone who came out said they had not been accepted but hung about to see if anyone would be. Well, shock and awe it was only me they wanted. The kid from Amble, the first from his family including his two brothers not to go 'doon tha pit', who had been written off by Quack as a 'dimwit', was he now really going to get to be a 'polis?' It looked like I might get a shot at it. I was the only one who was accepted and without any academic qualifications whatsoever. If it were now with so much bearing put on educational achievements, particularly in so much that a degree qualifies one to be accepted automatically into the police, I can only assume the opposite would occur and I'd be the only one not to be accepted.

My thoughts turned to the head and his continual references to the ex-head boy, of him being a cop in Amble and us almost being brainwashed into believing that he had achieved something we could never aspire to. He was held up as a role model, in much the same way an Olympic gold medallist is, as a hero. I thought how shocked the head, Quack and many of the other school staff would be if they heard I was to become a copper. As far as I know, they never did and I was not going back to tell them because I was now as disinterested in them as they appeared to have been in me.

I think what made me stand out from the rest that day, was a combination of a few things, my dictation/spelling, my British Rail reference, my confident interview displaying my common sense and my having left the NE to try and improve myself and at such a young age. I was still short of 18. I may also have been lucky in that Inspector Hollin had NE connections and that might have somewhat endeared me to him.

As I have said, I believe my true education started the moment I left school and by that I mean, I'd had several jobs in the past 3 years and worked with real down to earth folk. I'd gained confidence, in each experience at a new workplace and I had learned people skills. I believe that if you have common sense and people skills, anyone can become a good and effective cop. I have met many people with a degree but clearly, some were lacking in common sense. I may be biased but I truly believe that a degree only shows there is an ability to absorb information and that is pretty much it. As a cop, common sense in my book outperforms a degree, say in history, every time. Sadly, I never met anyone with a degree in common sense and until the day such a thing comes into being, guys like me will continue to struggle to have their true potential recognised.

As I boarded the train for my return to Worthing, I was again reminded of the ones I had 'played with' and left behind in Darlington. I had never had a train set but then acquired the real thing. I also never had a kids pedal police car but was now the real thing within my reach and to become my replacement toy and 'cops and robbers' the new game?

On the train, I spotted one of the 2 girls who had attended Oakland's House that day. I asked if I could join her and she said, "Yes." She was disappointed of course but was still cheerful and chatty. She was very attractive, with small features and well-groomed but what I noticed most was her poise in that she was calm and graceful. I wondered why she had not readily been accepted and that seemed odd to me and by odd, I don't mean I suspected anything untoward but I thought she would have been an ideal candidate.

Her name was Cathy and she lived in Brighton. We chatted all the way and awkward silences were never experienced in my company, for I took after my Mam in that respect and not my reserved Dad. I alighted from the train at Worthing and Cathy continued on her way to Brighton but that was not the last I would see of the lovely Cathy, for her phone number was now safely stored in my wallet.

It had been a good day I thought but not time yet to pat myself on the back. I had one more worrying hoop to jump through and that was the dreaded medical. Like my brother, Alan, who so much wanted to join the RAF as a pilot but failed on his eyesight, was my asthma going to do the same for me?

THE DREADED POLICE MEDICAL

My use of the asthma inhalers had increased over the years and I was reliant on them and if I were to be without one, it would psychologically trigger an attack. The frequent repeat prescription record would cause concern if spotted and I was sure it could well scupper my chances. So after weighing up the situation I decided to keep stum about it. It was a chance I thought I had to take.

I subsequently attended a ground floor doctor's surgery in Chichester with a very elderly doctor indeed. I quickly formed the opinion that the doctor urgently needed to see a doctor for he appeared to move cautiously as if in pain and his breathing was laboured. The sash window was opened at its widest and the net curtain was billowing in the wind, perhaps so the poor doctor might get as much fresh air as possible. People were walking past the open window on the busy pavement. I somewhat regretted my decision to keep quiet about my inhalers otherwise, I'd have compassionately offered the doctor a shot or two. As yet he had not spoken and had just beckoned to me to sit down.

He told me in a very loud voice to take off my shirt, Oh! Dear, he was deaf too. He then tapped my chest and back a couple of times with his bony fingers and then put the stethoscope on me. I suddenly thought, as I heard his chest wheezing way above mine ever had at its very worst, that I should be ok here as together with his deafness any lesser wheezes emanating from within me would be drowned out by his. He, without telling me to put my shirt on again, called out between wheezes, "Stand and drop your trousers." I hesitated for a second and thought I'll be naked and then it flashed through my mind, should he not take me out to dinner first? I looked at the open window, the blowing curtain and the people. What the hell, I dropped my trousers and as in the action of testing a peach for ripeness, he squeezed my undercarriage and indicated for me to dress. "A1, goodbye," he said.

I was relieved but I wondered how many corpses the good doctor had passed, as being also A1! I was out on my way within minutes when I realised he had only spoken/shouted about a dozen words during the time I was with him. Happily, my asthma was never to be mentioned throughout my service and apart from the odd sick day here and there, it was never to restrict my performance.

My family were pleased and proud of the bairn, 'Wor Tom is the Polis' but I was sad that my Dad was not around to witness my induction. I had always been called by my full name of Thomas by the family but gradually I got everyone to call me Tom. As I matured I always thought a lad from Amble and with a character such as mine was more suited to being a Tom, as opposed to a Thomas.

It was a few days since my medical when a problem arose in that Alan was to be transferred to Basingstoke on promotion within SPD, a subsidiary of Birds Eye. So the problem for me was, where was I going to live?

I START THE POLICE CADETS IN WORTHING AND I MOVE TO LIVE IN BRIGHTON

Alan called a meeting with Ray who was living in Woodingdean, Brighton and suggested it might be best for me if I were to go to him for a while. Somewhat reluctantly, it was agreed that would happen. I say reluctantly because that was the impression I got from Ray's wife, Liz, who became a very dominant figure and she made it clear that it was only a temporary arrangement. Liz was a totally different woman to Sylvia and I found her hard work to get along with, as many did.

Within a few weeks at the beginning of September 1967 and a month away from my 18th birthday, I said farewell to the lads at the factory and moved to Brighton. I then began the much longer commute every day to Worthing police station, where I had been posted. I wore a police cadet uniform, with a blue cap band and
130

blue 'West Sussex Constabulary' shoulder flashes. I cannot recall what my first month's salary was but I do know it was not more than the £10 per week I had earned at the factory but there was not a huge difference.

At first, I travelled to Worthing by bus from Woodingdean to Brighton rail station and then onto Worthing by train. Fortunately for me another cadet at Worthing, John Daniels, lived in Brighton and commuted daily on his Triumph Tiger Cub motorcycle. John was initially a learner rider but lady luck was on my side once again and as I had passed my test, I could legally accompany him as a pillion passenger. John was a really nice, reliable guy and so the arrangement worked well with me getting the bus to Brighton rail station where he would pick me up. He proved to be a competent and safe rider and not once did I have cause for concern.

At Worthing police station I worked 9 to 5 within the station and at first, on the switchboard. Callers must have thought from my accent that they had reached some far off land, perhaps where men wore wooden clogs, as I'd seen in Amble during bad weather!

Then I went into the general office and carried out basic tasks pretty much as I had at Darlington British Rail. I was not over-stretched mentally and the work was not difficult. The main thing was, everyone was accepting of me and my accent, helpful and pleasant. I was soon comfortable in the environment and excitedly happy.

MY WILD 18th BIRTHDAY

My 18th birthday, on 14 October 1967, I remember very clearly and instead of celebrating with my first legal pint, I spent most of the night sheltering from a wild storm behind a drystone wall, somewhere in the countryside of West Sussex. An all-night exercise had been arranged which involved a group of army cadets. They had to get from point A to point B and we police cadets had to apprehend them. I cannot remember much else about it, except two of our guys, had fallen into an open cesspit during the night. In the morning we had breakfast in a hall and were pleased to be out of the cold until the stinking hapless pair joined us. It wasn't easy to tell if the individuals were in dark blue police cadet overalls or army cadet khaki. No one was interested enough to hang about to find out whether they were 'us' or 'them' and it was by then completely immaterial because no one wanted to own them.

THE SNOW OF 1967

Every 2 weeks I attended a cadet training day, at Oakland's House Chichester. We had lectures on basic policing and I experienced drill on the parade ground and I found I was completely useless and lacked all sense of body coordination. Thank goodness we only did it a few times.

I was at such a day's training during the winter and shortly after I got there, that it started to snow heavily and I mean heavily. By noon it was decided to call a halt to the day's agenda and we were allowed to leave for home. I was one of those who had the furthest to go, a distance of 35 miles on the train to Brighton and then by bus to Woodingdean. I boarded the train and it departed without any let-up in snowfall. The journey was hampered by continual stoppages.

At coming up to 10 pm we still had not arrived at Brighton station. The train could not get there and it was diverted to Preston Park, a small station on the outskirts. I then walked the 3 or 4 miles to Woodingdean, across the open space and hill by the coast. The walk took me 2 hours and at times, I was up to my waist in drifting snow. I almost collapsed in through the door when I finally got home. The following day, Woodingdean was well and truly snowed in and I couldn't get to work. I will never forget that winters day in 1967.

SUSSEX POLICE AMALGAMATION AND I AM POSTED TO BRIGHTON

On the 1st January 1968, the 5 separate police forces within Sussex being, West Sussex, East Sussex, Brighton, Eastbourne and Hastings all amalgamated and became one, Sussex Police. I had asked to be posted to Brighton and that very considerately was granted and so on amalgamation day. I reported happy and excited for duty at Brighton, Johns Street, police station.

In the summer of that year for two weeks, I was sent on a residential lifeguard course with a couple of other cadets to Atlantic College, Llantwit Major, Wales, on the Bristol Channel. We bunked in the college as it was midterm and the student accommodation was vacant. We lived in swimsuits (not knitted) and shorts the whole time and we were kept busy with swimming, lifesaving coaching, canoeing, surfboarding and manning fast inshore inflatable lifeguard powerboats. My first real holiday I thought and I'm getting paid too. I loved it and came away with a gold medallion for personal survival and a bronze medallion for life-saving, which is why we were sent in the first place

I left the course and I did a week back at Brighton Police Station and I then went off to Bosham Harbour for a further two weeks, to learn how to sail a dinghy, more toys! Every day we were out on the water in the Mirage 3 man dinghies. The police owned a barge that was moored on the banks of the harbour. It was called the Gerald Daniels and had been donated to the Sussex Police by Gerald's parents when he died in police service. It was a large vessel and had a separate bunk room for the girls and it accommodated us all comfortably. We had all our fantastic meals cooked for us and this time I cared not one jot if anyone called out 'Curry-free' because for once everyone was 'in the same boat ' and all were entitled to free dinners!

From day one, we had a ball. We were all the same age and young. The days and long light evenings were filled with laughter and teasing and dare I say, flirting with the girls. I continued in my role as the class clown and it appeared to be appreciated by all, including Inspector Maurice Clyde, who was in charge of our cadet training and was with us every day. I liked the Inspector, he was a kind and understanding man and I know he liked me because I remember what he wrote on my report which I had sight of. He wrote, 'Cadet Curry has a razor-sharp sense of humour and is popular with his colleagues.' Praise indeed I thought and enough for it to stick in mind for 50+ years.

At the end of that two weeks, what with the previous course and being on the water all day long, I was the most tanned and fittest I had ever been in my young life but unfortunately, I still needed to use the asthma inhaler.

I was never as happy lodging with Ray, as I was at Alan's but that was not Ray's fault, it was the temperamental behaviour of his wife Liz. Ray and I never knew when she would suddenly lose her cool over something of no great importance. She would scream, throw stuff, rant and rave, causing alarm to anyone witnessing the scene and with the sole purpose of getting her way. Ray was an easy-going, anything for a quiet life sort of guy and very much like our Dad. He was a good, reliable and conscientious worker.

Life outside the home moved along nicely. I spent time with Cathy and enjoyed her company during the summer. We spent days on Brighton beach, weather permitting and we had fun together. I had my normal two weeks holiday and so I figured I'd had 6 weeks that year as I looked upon the two courses as holidays.

I continued with my driving school lessons in a Morris 1100. After about ten lessons and thinking about the £1 for each, I applied for a test, against my driving instructor's advice in saying I was not ready. He was right, I was wrong. A short while later, I applied again but this time, I was a bit unfortunate because at a crossroads and when turning right, the car in front stalled and then moved off on amber leaving me stranded in the middle. I applied again straight away and this time I passed. I did not look for a car immediately because I wanted to save a bit more and buy a decent second-hand one for cash.

For the next few months, I carried out various duties at Brighton police station, working in the general office, as at Worthing and then in the C.I.D office, answering the many phones. I then went out on uniform foot patrol and motor car patrol in the town, (a city now) always with the most experienced officers. I will not go into the various incidents I attended but they were all the general run of the mill everyday type of jobs the police deal with. I loved the hustle and bustle and atmosphere of Brighton, together with the fast pace of policing needed to maintain good order. I wanted to be posted there as a PC but it never happened.

CHAPTER 7

APPOINTED AS A POLICE CONSTABLE AND TRAINING COLLEGE

So came my 19th birthday and my appointment as a police constable which was not automatic and each cadet had to be finally assessed as to suitability. My appointment went through smoothly without any problem and so 'Wor Tomis the Polis' was official and I was now Police Constable AC980 Thomas William Curry of the Sussex Police.

PC AC980 Tom Curry.

There then followed a few weeks before I went off for 12 weeks of residential initial training, at the Police College at Sandgate, Kent. During the interim period, I was allowed quite a unique privilege. Although I was not officially sworn in as a constable, I was allowed to continue on outside patrol duty, wearing my PC's uniform but always in the company of an experienced PC.

It was at the beginning of November 1968, that I arrived at the police college at Sandgate, Kent. It stood in its own grounds and the main building was of grey stone and had the look of having been a stately home at one time. There were also temporary buildings that were classrooms. PC's from various southern forces attended including from the Channel Islands. I was in a room with 3 others, including Alan Trussler from Sussex, who I mentioned previously.

I think there might have been 30 in my class from various forces. Throughout the course, we received training and lectures in every aspect of police work, including mock incidents when we played all the roles, with a student PC acting as the PC out on the streets. We would be called upon to write witness statements and in a mock set up of a court, we would give evidence and be cross-examined by the training sergeant taking the role of the defending counsel.

I performed well both practically and in exams and was never rebuked or criticised from the beginning to the end of the course. I was about the middle of the class in exam results and that had always been my placing at all stages of my education and cadet training. Once again I did not study in my own time and achieved my results purely on classwork. However, I did have a plan this time and that was, I had a seat right at the front and gave my full concentration to the training sergeant and followed his every word. I was not going to mess this chance up and Tom Curry the 'class clown' was firmly in hiding and even Interpol would not be able to flush him out!

As soon as class finished though, when others continued to bury their noses in their books, I was back to my old self, joking and having fun. I was always one of the first in the bar and I was there until closing but not overindulging, just joking with the lads. Lots of them did not stop studying until nearly closing time but that was never for me. I never had to either, as I could maintain acceptable results with my simple M.O and relying on what I still consider my exceptional memory. Although I wanted to better myself, I never had the driving ambition to get to the top of any tree. So I am not going to bore either myself or the reader, in any further detail regarding classwork/training and so with that, we'll move on to some fun stuff.

DRILL WITH WILL ON THE HILL

The main thing I remember about Sandgate is someone who always warms my heart and brings a smile to my face when I remember him and he has the same effect on all who I have ever come in contact with. That person is the most unlikely person you might expect and that is, the drill sergeant, Will Squires, known to us lads as Will the Drill. He was in his late 50s, a big man with a red face, twinkling eyes and an impish grin. He was overweight and with a beer belly but when he was on the drill square and he came to attention, he would be transformed into as smart a drill instructor as any man, who ever graced a parade square. He knew his business and no question about it, which was just as well because I was going to test his skills, for sure.

As I mentioned earlier, I first found out at cadet drill that I was useless but we didn't drill with any intensity and so it was only at Sandgate, that I found out that I was the worst of the worst. I truly do lack any form of body coordination whatsoever. It didn't seem to matter how many times I told myself to step off with my left leg whilst swinging my right arm forward. Somehow along the way, I always ended up either swinging both arms forward and back at the same time or awkwardly marching whilst swinging my left arm forward in unison with my left leg and then vice versa with the right leg and right arm. Try both and you will get what I mean. All the others picked it up quite quickly but I never did. Alan Trussler used to do it with me in the corridor or room. I am sure he thought I was putting it on but not me, it was genuine. I wanted a quiet life for now and not for there to be any focus of attention on me, for whatever reason.

Time after time, Will would stop the parade because of me and I'd be stood with the others at attention in full uniform with helmet, on the parade square. Will, would come to me carrying his pace stick under his arm. He'd tap me gently under my privates with the stick, saying in a quiet voice, "What's a matter with you, Spike? (He called everyone, Spike.) Have you got house bricks for bollocks?" I'd say, "No, sarge." He'd say, "Well, why are you marching like a pregnant duck?" or other such sayings. He'd say either, "Watch me" or "You stand there and watch the lads."

When he thought it was time to stamp his authority because he was being monitored as well, he might say, "Right that's it. It's drill on the hill." and he would march us to quite a steep hill within the grounds. He'd then march us up and down a couple of times and then he'd say maybe, "You aren't quite getting this, are you? OK traffic signals for bubble cars, get down." So we'd have to crouch down on the steep hill in full uniform, a helmet too, with knees bent balancing and up on our toes. He'd instruct us to carry out hand signals as if directing traffic as we were crouched. He deemed it to be specifically for bubble cars.

Whilst we were at the college, we had to keep a pocketbook up to date, just like we'd have to do out on the street, with times and
140

lectures etc., just for practice. At the start of one drill session, he said, "The superintendent has had a word with me because he did a random check of one of your pocketbooks. You know who you are Spike! He found an entry he didn't think was funny. It read 3 pm Drill with Will. Now I'm going to add 3 more words to that, so it will now read, 3 pm Drill with Will on the Hill. Now get up there at the double!"

It was all tongue in cheek. Once we did a bit he'd say, "Now do you want some more or do you want to chip in for the dogs for the blind and then have a lemonade?" and the reply would always be "Dogs for the Blind and a lemonade, sarge." "Ok, see you right away in my office," he would say.

Now let me explain, it might be any charity, not just Dogs for the Blind and he did not have an office, he worked from the bar/area, which he ran. He also was the first aid instructor. In the corridor at the main entrance were scores of receipts pinned to a notice board from every charity under the sun. Will had collected thousands of pounds over the years for a multitude of charities and he'd been at the college a long time. The recipient charities must have thought coppers were the most generous people on earth.

Will was holding a gun to our heads every single day, many days two or three times, i.e. 'Do you want another half an hour of drill or make a charity donation for.........and break early for a lemonade or do you want to hear about drill or first aid?" Of course every time we elected to give up a couple of bob and break early for a lemonade and it was limited to lemonade through the day. It enhanced the bar takings too and so everyone gained including us, but not financially of course.

Then when he came around for the donation, he had another saying, "Only snow or out we go again!" That meant no copper, only silver coins. You could not get away without donating by saying, "I haven't got any change," because Will had the till keys and access to all the cash. He had it all sewn up. He could virtually call a halt anytime he liked and he did many times. The bar area was away from the main classrooms and there was a large room alongside the bar, where Will gave his lectures on either drill or first aid.

I recall one evening when Will arranged a film showing and I watched Zulu for the first time. I loved the story, the regimentation, the red tunics, the scenery and the Zulus too. It became my most favourite film of all time. I have watched it scores of times since and so much so that I know all the dialogue. Every time I see it I think of where I saw it first, Will and the course.

We were inspected once a week by the overseeing superintendent, a man who was aloof and humourless. He would inspect us on the parade ground and he'd often tell a man his boots needed more attention because we had to 'bull' (shine) the toe caps. Bull is army chat for bullshit. Will would be immediately behind the Supt. and he would say in a harsh voice, "You come and see me in my office at 8 pm and bring the boots with you" and would give a wink. We all knew what that meant except the superintendent. As I said, Will's office was the bar, which he ran every evening, always with a couple of volunteers/ press-ganged lads to help serve, which then freed Will to consume large amounts of beer and tell humorous yarns.

Now when the guy with the boots arrived Will took them and disappeared into a back room, where he put his somewhat lucrative sideline into operation. In the room, he had his boot bulling kit, a gas ring and canister, tin of black boot polish and a teaspoon. He'd heat the polish on the spoon and use the back of the spoon to bull the boots. After years of practice, he was a master of the skill and the boots were soon perfect. Of course, his work did not come free of charge and Will received the price of two pints of beer. The arrangement suited both parties especially Will, who had a guaranteed continual stream of customers to ensure he never went thirsty every night. The next time the superintendent did the inspection he might say, "That's better." Will would pass, wink and grin.

Will's other job was first aid training, which was very important to us Sussex guys because our force insisted that each one of us had to have a first-aid certificate. Will held his lectures in the room adjacent to the bar. We never did get a full lecture from him because he seemed to start with all the best of intentions in the world but then he'd just go off script and end up telling us about his police and war experiences, which enthralled all of us about to begin. He might even just open up the bar and we would buy lemonade and have a surreptitious free period.

As the course began to draw nearer to its conclusion, many of us started to get worried that come examination day we would know nothing about first aid. Anytime it was mentioned Will said something like, "In past years only one PC failed and that was because he forgot his name." Meaning it was not the first aid he failed on but on a technicality. We could not understand Will's confidence because first aid can cover a lot of ground. We knew a female GP came to the college and would verbally test each one of us individually and not only that but there was a practical on bandaging.

A week before the examination day and with panic setting in, Will decided to let us all into his secret. A lady doctor would arrive and each one of us would be taken in turn and asked 3 first aid questions. Then she would instruct you to go and bandage a mock patient for a particular injury. Well on the face of it, that was not going to help anyone, until he told us the following; he provided the doctor with the list of the questions she was to ask and she always worked straight down the list asking each man his 3 questions. He would tell us our 3 questions AND answers before we went in.

As far as the bandaging was concerned, after she asked the 3 questions, she told you what bandage she wanted you to apply. Then you went to the back of the room and applied the bandage on Will, while he whispered instructions and wriggled into the bandaging. After she had asked the next man his questions, she quickly checked Will wearing the bandaging and so on, until all was done. Will said, "Don't forget she wants to get away from here as fast as she can."

On the day and shortly before the doctor arrived, Will took another one of his 'snow only' only collections and this time it was for the visiting doctor. Sure enough, an elderly lady doctor arrived and I was reminded of the one I'd seen for my medical. It seemed the police liked to employ elderly semi-retired doctors and I found that to be the case so many times. Before the start of the proceedings and in front of us all, Will addressed the doctor and it went something like this, "On behalf of the lads, we would like to thank you most sincerely doctor, for giving up your busy time and coming today for this important matter. As a token of their deep appreciation, the lads would like to present you with, this bunch of flowers and this box of chocolates." Well, it was a decent bunch of flowers and a big box of chocolates too.

Well the sly old fox Will, eh? He was crafty enough to do the presentation before she did her bit and not after. So imagine, how could she fail anyone, even if it wasn't a fiddle? Anyway, it got underway and it went exactly as Will had said and we all got our first-aid certificate.

THE COLDITZ ESCAPE PLAN

Apart from the marching, the other thing I struggled with, as I had anticipated, was the cross country runs. Fortunately, there was one guy there from the Surrey force, a Welshman and of course he was known as Taffy. He was older than the rest of us and a typical tubby, jolly guy. He laughed hysterically at every one of my many jokes, his large belly going up and down as he did so. He was in the next room to me and I'd gotten to know him quite well even before a run and we agreed to do them together. He was overweight and when he had the running kit on, he did look comical. His shirt didn't reach his shorts and left part of his belly exposed, which hung over the shorts. He wore black ankle socks and had a large tattoo of a topless model on the side of one lower leg.

I teamed up with him for the first run and we were in for a shock because it was a lot further than we thought it would be. For the life of me, I cannot recall the distance in miles. So we set off at a snail's pace, which very soon reduced to that of an injured snail. I looked over at Taffy, to see him produce his baccy pouch from the pocket inside his shorts and was rolling a cigarette. On seeing this I said, holding an imaginary microphone up to his face, "Tom Curry. BBC news and how long have you been a keep fit merchant?" he again laughed hysterically, which turned into a coughing bout. I laughed too, not at the joke but at Taffy and I produced my inhaler from a similar pocket inside my shorts. I asked, Taffy if he thought the pocket was specifically for baccy and inhalers and he laughed and coughed at the same time.

It was getting late and we were well behind and Taffy said, "Sod it, I'm getting the bus." I said, "We haven't got any money." He produced a note from his baccy pouch and I think it was a 10 bob note. So we got on a bus and I remember the driver said, "Next time, make sure you have the right money for the fare." I said to Taffy, "If this carries on, it might be cheaper to get a bus pass!" We both laughed.

146

We got off at the stop just before the college and I said, "We'll have to look knackered." We must have realised at the same time that we didn't need to pretend and we both started to laugh at the same moment, which knackered us even more. When we entered the building, one of the duty squad PC's (another student) told us that the PT instructor had said that we had to not bother changing and go straight in for our supper, as everyone else had finished theirs and we were holding the staff up. So we entered the mess hall and the two of us were the only ones in there. The PT instructor wasn't critical of us and he just said something like, "Where the hell have you two been?" and shook his head. We must have fought off any impulse to say that the bus was running late and so we said nothing!

Taffy and I had a discussion and we decided we had to come up with something because we couldn't go through this every time. The problem was each time during a run a marshal, another student, would be somewhere along the course and would stamp each runner with an ink stamp but the part of the body stamped would vary i.e. right hand, left leg etc. We both thought about trying to get the marshal's job but that would not be possible as there was only one and it was someone different each run.

What we came up with, was we could stamp ourselves if we got ink and a makeshift stamp, which we could fashion out of a raw potato. The stamp was always the same just a star shape and we could smudge it anyway. The canteen women were lovely and many of us, just for a bit of fun flirted or joked with them and they took it in good spirit i.e., "Hello Doris, you're looking exceptionally lovely today" etc. They had also laughed with me and Taffy when we were late. So before the next run, we took them a box of Quality Street and let a couple of them into the secret. They seemed to enjoy the idea of the fun/secrecy of it all. We asked for a potato which we carved into a star shape and we found an ink pad that could be temporarily borrowed from the student duty squad, just for the period of the run and until such time that we got our own.

 Now, how were we going to put it into action? The plan would be as follows; we would run out but duck into the bushes that ran all around the grounds. We'd sit in the bushes by the kitchen where the canteen women were. We'd wait there and one of our mates, a good runner, when he returned, would come and tell us where he'd been stamped. We'd stamp ourselves and near the end, we'd run out. I told Taffy that I thought it best if we didn't win!

Taffy and I found the prospect fun and exciting and from then on we referred to the college as, Colditz Castle. We fantasised that we were there and planning an escape. At one stage, I borrowed a dessert spoon from the canteen and back in our room, I produced it saying, "We have to have a plan B. Tonight after lights out, we start a tunnel." I was in my element and started referring to the instructors as the 'goons' as the POW's did in Colditz when they mentioned the German guards. We talked and laughed about forging identity papers and making maps of Sandgate, getting access to train timetables and making civvy clothes out of police uniforms etc. Thinking of my brother's glider, I suggested we build

148

one, as they'd done in Colditz but we decided it would not work as the college roof was not high enough for a launch!

In all, it was jolly good fun and certainly broke the monotony of our free time. Most importantly, it would cause us to avoid the dreaded cross country runs. We used the plan many times and went undetected. We sat in the bushes and the canteen women giggled about it and handed out mugs of tea and we handed back sweets.

I remember one occasion when it rained. Taffy and I huddled under an umbrella that was handed out to us, whilst we drank tea and Taffy smoked his roll-ups. Had we been discovered, I'd have pleaded guilty and asked for a further 10 offences to be taken into consideration. In mitigation, I'd have asked that our great enterprise be taken into account. I absolutely loved orchestrating that schoolboy wheeze, which of course was all about avoiding Taffy's and my wheeze!

END OF COURSE

On our final night, we had a big party and we had a whip-round for our lovely Will the Drill and he was visibly upset, which in turn visibly upset many of us.

The passing out parade was held the day we left. Will asked me if any of my family were coming and I told him, "No, sarge." I said it was too far for my Mam to come and I didn't want any fuss. Will said, "Don't worry Spike, you can do the car park" and so that's what I did. I wasn't on the passing out parade, which I was pleased about.

We were to learn later, that poor Will had lost his wife a few years earlier and had no family. He had done 30 years of service but had asked if he could stay on for a bit. Somewhat sadly, it seemed that we were all his family, on this course, the previous course and the next one to come too.

The next course after ours, Will finally retired and got a job as a court usher somewhere in Kent. Shortly after that, he was featured in the national papers because he sprayed some hell's angels, who were sitting at the back of the court, with fresh air spray. Good old lovely, Will!

I had thoroughly enjoyed the course and I was happy with my middle of the road results, which I had always enjoyed without a great deal of effort. It proved that I was not out of my depth academically, taking into account my basic NE pit village education and at least I now knew I could hold my own against the rest of the competition.

During the course, I had been told that I would be posted pending my results, to Crawley a town I knew nothing whatsoever about. Then after not being able to find accommodation for me, it was changed to Worthing, which I was more than happy to return to.

Throughout the 12 weeks of the course I had returned to Ray and Liz most weekends but now I would be moving out, which suited all. I had lost touch with the lovely Cathy and decided not to rekindle our friendship, as I would not be living in Brighton.

Around this time, I bought my first car, a black Hillman Minx. It was second-hand but in great condition. I bought it privately and paid cash for it. It served me well and proved to be reliable and was a good purchase.

CHAPTER 8

POSTED TO WORTHING AGAIN

At about the beginning of February 1969, together with Alan Trussler my mate, I was posted once again to Worthing. The police station or 'nick' at that time was in Union Place right in the town centre. Adjacent to but in a separate building, was the single men's section house. I thought I was more fortunate than Alan because I knew the people at the nick and a bit about the town. At the nick, we were given two addresses in the town centre, both of which offered digs. I said that I'd take the Upper High Street one and Alan took the other. The section house for single men and women was full at that time. I knew my address was nearer to the nick and was only a few hundred yards away but Alan's was about ½ a mile distant.

I went to introduce myself to the landlady and Alan went off to meet his. Mine occupied the 1st floor of a Victorian house and she rented out the ground floor to a couple, the man I was to get to know quite well and liked. He was a taxi driver who worked permanent nights and was called Roy. There were to be many cold wintery nights when he would welcome me into his office, always with a warm smile and an even warmer welcome cup of tea.

My landlady, Mrs Gladwell was the sweetest old lady that one could ever meet. She was well into her 70s I would guess, tiny, slim and always wore a hat and I never saw her without it, indoors or out. She greatly reminded me of the endearing, sweet little old lady, Mrs Willberforce, in the 1955 Ealing Studios comedy, The Ladykillers. Elderly actress Katie Johnson played the part. The flat was clean and tidy but all furnishings were old. I would be occupying a room at the rear. She said that she could not supply any food but I was welcome to tea and biscuits at any time. She would provide bed linen and change the bed as and when but I'd have to do my own washing. She said the rent would be £2 and 10 shillings a week, which I thought was a steal. It was clear she was very fond of the police and I was to learn later that she only took police lodgers, as it gave her a sense of security. My food was no problem, there was a good police canteen at the nick but I would not be, Curry-free! My washing, I could do at the laundrette. I was very happy with the arrangements. Alan Trussler was not. He got full board and I forget exactly what he paid but it was around £6 a week. Mrs Gladwell was always sweet, whilst Alan's landlady was not. I recall he told me that she saw he had one bar of an electric fire on and said if that were to become a habit, he'd need to pay another 10 bob a week.

So having settled into my new digs, I reported to the nick at 9 am along with Alan and we spent that day being shown the ropes so

152

to speak and meeting the chiefs. I did not feel awkward as Alan would be being the new boy because I knew the place and most of the people. The next morning I was to join my section, who were on early turn, 6 am to 2 pm. You did 7 x 6 am to 2 pm shifts from Friday, finishing on Thursday at 2 pm. Then off until 10 pm Monday. Then, 7 x night shifts being from, 10 pm to 6 am, finishing on Monday morning. Then off until Wednesday 2 pm and then 7 x 2 pm to 10 pm late shifts, finishing 10 pm the following Tuesday and off until 6 am Friday and so on. You were always expected to be in attendance and ready for duty 10 minutes before the shift began.

I joined 'A' section consisting of an inspector, 3 sergeants and about 15 PCs. My inspector was a gruff ill-mannered man who I learnt to avoid. However, one of the 3 sergeants was Joe Rowland, who I would grow to look upon as a role model and father figure. Joe was a practical cop, level headed with bags of common sense. He was a man's man and supervised not through fear but by being respected. He also had a sense of fun and would join in on a joke or a jolly jape.

I recall hearing a story several times of what Joe had done when he was a rural constable and living in a police house. It was late one night and Joe had gone to bed as he was on an early shift in the morning. He heard a loud banging on his front door. He opened the door wearing his pyjamas and saw a local greengrocer who said, "I've had my bike pinched." Joe said, "Well what do you expect me to do about it? This isn't a police station and I'm not on duty. Ring the police station." The guy said grumpily, "You call yourself a policeman!" and walked off.

That was not the end because Joe visited the greengrocer's home on his way to work early in the morning and banged on his door. The guy opened his bedroom window and called out, "What do you want?" Joe said, "I want a cabbage and some spuds." The guy said, "I'm not open yet!" Joe said, "You call yourself a greengrocer!" and he walked off. I think Joe had proven his point that 'what is good for the goose is good for the gander!'

I cannot mention or describe everyone in this book because we need to move the narrative along with interesting topics but suffice it to say I met and worked with some great guys.

For the first few weeks, I was assigned to another PC, (later Sergeant) Paddy Cashman and he showed me how you were expected to work a beat, pointing out local criminals and any pubs etc. that should be paid particular interest. I was also taken and introduced to 'tea spots' where a PC might be welcomed and be offered a tea and short respite from the cold. Paddy did not have a great deal of service with the police but as an ex-marine he was streetwise. He became a lifelong close friend until he sadly died a few years back.

After this relatively short period, I was then allocated my town centre beat. From then on I was on my own but normally always in contact via radio, if I required any advice or assistance. The personal radios in those days could be temperamental and would lose contact sometimes. There were a few occasions where we had to revert to the old-style communication of points, where at a particular time you would be called at a public telephone box but those moments gladly were both rare and brief. On such occasions, my police whistle on a chain, which I carried throughout my service, was the only means of sounding an alarm or summoning assistance. Little wonder that police killed on duty in the days without a radio, I believe, still outnumber those in modern times.

A SHOCK REUNION

I had only been at Worthing a couple of weeks and on or about the 1st March 1969, I was on an early turn shift. (6 am to 2 pm.) A sergeant said to me that I had to watch a male prisoner in the cells who was in for suspected murder. It's quite normal for the police, when a person is in custody on such a serious matter, to have a 24-hour watch kept on him/her so that nothing happens such as self-harm or suicide. In this case, the cell door was to be left open and I was to sit immediately outside that door, so I could see the prisoner at all times. Of course, the cellblock entrance/exit door would be locked with me inside. I had to go to the cell block straight away to relieve the current PC watcher, who was going off from night duty. I had to note in my pocketbook everything the suspect said or did. I was told nothing more about the man or the case.

This would be the first time I would come in direct contact with a suspected murderer but not the last. I went to the cellblock and took over from the PC who was then able to leave the area. I saw that the prisoner was laid on the bed and he appeared to be asleep. I did not go right up to him but remained outside the cell. His cell door was ajar and a chair in place for me to have a direct view of him.

About an hour later, he began to stir and he got to his feet. When he saw me he said," Hello Tom." I instantly recognised him as he had me. It was Richard Bari Tuck the little guy I had worked with at the Shoreham factory, only about 18 months previously. The conversation that took place is as close as I can get to it because this was about 50 years ago. I said, "Hello Bari. I was not expecting to see you." He said, "I've been an idiot." I said, "I don't even know what you are supposed to have done." He said, "I've murdered an old woman." Thinking I should say not too much. I just said, "Have you?" He said," Yes, I did it. What do you think I'll get?" I thought I better not say, 'life.' So I said, "It's up to the judge." He said, "What's the maximum I could get?" I said," It does carry a life sentence but that does not mean that you'll get that." He said, "Right." I said," Look, Bari, I have to speak to my sergeant on the phone and so you go back into the cell for a bit."

He went back into the cell and I reached for the phone and rang the sergeant. I said, "Can you come down here? I need to speak to you." Of course, he came without any hesitation. I whispered to him what had gone on and he said that he would get someone to take my place, which was done within minutes. Before I left the cellblock I said to Bari, "I've got to go now Bari, I might not see you again."

156

I thought this is a good start. Everyone's going to think I'm the mate of a murderer! I left and never saw Bari again. One thing that stuck in my mind all these years, was seeing his shoes outside the cell door, which is normal practice, they were size 6. Richard Bari Tuck was just 19 years old when he was given a life sentence.

The brief details of his crime were that he had a room at a doss of a bed-sit at The Moreland's Hotel mainly occupied by social security claimants. He'd been having a sexual relationship with an 88-year-old female alcoholic, Florence Beatrice Early. He had been drinking and in her room, he strangled and horribly sexually violated her. He wrote, 'Whore,' across her chest in lipstick and left. The body was discovered the next day and the CID were called. Lipstick marks were found on the light switch, left behind when it had been switched off. All the occupants were seen in turn and when it came to Bari he still had lipstick under his fingernails. Bari was nicked.

In1987, he was found dead in his cell at HMP Lewes. His death was from natural causes and he was just 37 years old when he died. What a waste of a young life but not forgetting the sad demise of his victim too.

I ATTEND THE FIRST OF MANY SUDDEN DEATHS

Every PC will be able to remember the first sudden-death they attended. I have double the reason to do so because it was a double death. I had only been out working a beat on my own for a few months when I was sent to a ground floor flat where the elderly couple had not been seen for a few days. The curtains were closed, it was during the day and that I thought looked ominous. I managed to slip the catch on a sash cord window and climbed into a bedroom. The centre light was on and there were two single beds. Unfortunately, in one was an elderly man dressed in his pyjamas and he was dead. I searched the rest of the house and in the kitchen/diner, on the floor, was a fully dressed elderly lady who was also dead. Next to her was a telephone and a bottle on its side of prescribed tablets, in the name of the male occupant. The cap was off and some of the tablets were strewn about.

Now a double death like this is very unusual and should in my mind always be treated as suspicious. I knew this would need further scrutiny by those of a higher rank than me. My starting point was to call for my section uniform sergeant to attend, which he duly did. He agreed that it should be escalated further and the CID were requested to attend. It is not necessary to go into any further detail as to what went on next and who else attended. It is sufficient to say, it was decided that both the deceased had died of natural causes and the post mortem confirmed that to be so.

What appeared to have taken place, was that it was night time i.e. the lights were still on. The husband had gone to bed first. Later his wife was also about to turn in when she found her husband dead. She rushed to get his tablets and at the same time was probably about to telephone for an ambulance but she had a heart attack and also died. I thought how sad it was but then maybe they would have wanted to go at the same time.

Right from day one, I decided that if there was any doubt in my mind whatsoever, I would preserve the scene as a crime scene and treat the death as being suspicious, until I was 100% convinced that it was not. I was always to follow that premise. If it later transpired I was wrong and it was a natural death, then I would not then be open to criticism, as I would be if I had cause for suspicion and did not preserve the scene and thus lost vital forensic evidence for a murder enquiry. However, you will read further on that not everyone within the police service followed the same guidelines.

I have dealt with many sudden deaths, in my lengthy police career but I do not wish to recount the details of them all. What I do want to say is this, although I have seen many deceased, attended too many fatal traffic accidents, post mortems and murder scenes, I am an emotional, sensitive, compassionate man and can be reduced to tears by a sad film, where the fictional character might be killed or dies or an underdog does good tale.

So for a long time, I wondered how it was that I was able to compose myself to execute my duty in dealing with death without breaking down. It took a long time for me to come up with a plausible answer. I came upon it when I thought about the fact that I had not and never will, visit a loved one and view them after death. I would find that far too harrowing and best avoided. I want to remember my loved ones as and when they were alive.

So the answer has to be, that in all the deaths I have attended, I have never known that person when they were alive. I never saw them talk, move, smile, laugh or do anything a live person does

159

and so I have never known their character. That gave me the emotional detachment that I needed to function in my chosen work. I know for instance, that I could never have been a male nurse because they have physical contact and a type of relationship that will be undoubtedly bond-forming, irrespective of how minute that might be. To do that and then perhaps the next day, find their bed empty would be too much for me.

Now to continue with my story, in the first few months, most of my jobs were pretty mundane and the normal run of the mill general stuff such as traffic offences, drunks and taking petty crime reports, including vandalism. I particularly loath the crime of vandalism because it has no motive, it is just simply the deliberate damage, often of expensive public property or that of some hard-working person, for the sake of it. All other crimes have a motive, theft is personal gain, assault mostly for revenge and sexual offences are for personal sexual gratification. So I was always happy to catch a vandal. I was pretty much learning my trade on the hoof and I was eager to prove my worth and as luck would have it I would not have to wait long to become recognised by my peers as a young cop who had potential as a 'thief-taker'

I MOVE INTO THE SINGLE MEN'S SECTION HOUSE

I had only been with Mrs Gladwell a few short months when a vacancy in the section house arose and I was happy to take it.

Let's take a break from the heavy stuff and I can maybe lighten the mood with hopefully a humorous story, as my thirst for a laugh never quenches. In the single men's section house, I had my

160

own room and there were about a dozen men's rooms and along the corridor, 3 for women. These were all first floor rooms and on the ground floor was a canteen, which everyone at the nick used. There was no canteen staff over the Christmas break and so we single guys retained access to the canteen to be able to cook.

Just after Christmas Day, whilst using the canteen I spotted a large Christmas pudding which had been unused and I guess had been forgotten. It had been left standing unprotected. By the New Year, it was still there and had taken on a sad and mouldy look. So feeling sorry for it, I decided to adopt it and keep it as a 'pet' for a while in my room. So I took a rolling pin and rolled it out until it was about 18 inches long and about 3 inches in circumference. I then slipped a piece of heavy-duty cardboard under it and that way it was easily transported to my room.

I cleared the top of my chest of drawers and placed the cardboard with my pet on the top. I had already decided on a plan for its use but I would wait for the best time of execution. A couple of evenings later, it seemed a good time because a number of the other residents were in a room, just chatting and I wanted as big an audience as I could muster.

I saw a young cadet, a pasty and lanky lad, come out of the toilets, walk along the corridor and join the others. I quickly shot out to the toilet with my pet in tow. Very carefully I lifted and placed him into the bowl of the toilet headfirst, with his tail just overlapping and resting on the top of the toilet seat. I made sure that the end in the water, just disappeared up out of sight into the U bend and so if you didn't know, you had no way of telling how much further it went. The end resting on the seat, with my fingers I gave it a nice little neat taper, ending in a fine point. All this had only taken a few seconds. I hid the cardboard and went quickly to the room where the group were congregating.

I tried to look shocked and interrupted them by saying, "Who's just come out of the bog?" The skinny cadet said, "Me, why?" I said, "Why, are you joking or what? You can get in there and clean that up!" He said, "Clean what up? I haven't caused any mess." I said, "Right all of you, just come and look and see what you reckon." So with that, we all troop off to the toilet. Well, when I pushed the door in, even though I say it myself, my pet looked magnificent in his new setting. There was a mixture of gasps, 'Chrrrrist's and bloooody hell's' and expletives all at once. Some moved closer for a better look but then shied away as if it might leap out at any second. I saw a couple of the guys look the skinny cadet up and down as if in envy or admiration. Meanwhile, he was pleading his innocence and kept repeating, "That's not down to me. Honestly, that is not down to me!" I said," You can get it cleaned up or I'm reporting you to the superintendent." I gave him one last chance and said, "Are you going to clean it up or not?" He said, "No, I am not because it's not down to me." He looked as if was going to cry and so I said, "Well somebody has to get rid of it." I quickly leapt forward grabbed it by its tail and threw it into the bowl and pulled the chain. Well, there were further gasps of, 'Chrrrrist's and bloooody hell's and I'm going to be sick's!' We all fell about laughing, including the cadet, when I said," It's just a manky old Christmas pud!"

162

MY MATE MICK

On moving into the section house, I met a great guy called Mick Richardson, who was also a resident. He was a PC at Shoreham, just a few miles along the coast. His parents ran a farm at Burwash in East Sussex. I spent time with him there, riding horses Bobby and Cilla. At about the age of 21, Mick joined The Bermuda police and moved out there. His girlfriend Val, an Aussie by birth but they had met in the UK, followed him. After a while, they returned to the UK, to be married. I was honoured to be Mick's best man at their wedding in Lewes. I was fortunate to holiday in Bermuda and I stayed with the lovely couple, on two separate occasions.

After Mick had completed a 5-year tour of duty, he and Val moved to Canberra, Australia and brought up their two sons and daughter there. Mick joined the Canberra police and retired after 25 years. In his time Mick has driven coaches and diesel goods trains and still does part-time.

During the 50 years that we have known each other, we have spent relatively little time together. However, our bonding is such that we may not see each other for many years but as soon as we meet up again, immediately we are at ease in each other's company.

Unfortunately, I never got to work with Mick. I regret that we did not get to spend more time together. Mick is the finest man I have ever had the pleasure of meeting and I have met many fine men. I love both him and his lovely wife.

They say, 'Join the navy and see the world.' Mick did it courtesy of the police.

MY FIRST BURGLAR AND COMMENDATION

At about 8 pm on the evening of 25th July 1969, I was off duty and in the section house and nothing that interested me was on TV. I decided to go for a walk on my own. It was getting dark and I walked along Union place. At the other end of the road and on the opposite side to the nick, there was an Art College, surrounded by bushes, where students attended evening classes, often until very late at night. It was not unusual to see people coming and going at that hour. I saw a young guy come out of the college entrance and walk off casually, pretty much as normal, like the rest of those exiting. I just thought he did not look quite right, not an arty/beatnik type. I had still retained an interest in art from my schooldays but my skills, not being practised were on the wane but that had not prevented me from taking an interest in the types attending the college.

 He could have had a multitude of other reasons to be there of course but I decided to speak to him. I caught up with him and introduced myself. I asked him if he attended the college. He said that he did not but he'd gone into the bushes to relieve himself. That was somewhat believable but I was not letting him go without satisfying myself that he was genuine, not now I had stopped him. I asked if he had any ID on him he said he had not. I didn't like that either. He was wearing a big dark coloured anorak. It was then I asked him to show me what he had on him. He refused and said that he'd done nothing wrong. I said, "Then you shouldn't mind letting me see then." He told me he was going. I must have thought, in for a penny in for a pound, here goes and grabbed his arm. He struggled and we had quite a violent tussle and I felt something metal inside his coat. That was enough for me. I went for it and we fell to the floor. I got the better of him and pulled his coat open. He had a crowbar and a bulky canvas bank bag. He was now in my bag and I had nicked the first of my many burglars!

I took him to the nick and there was great excitement. I was soon to discover that it was not every day, an off duty cop, on his own, nicks a burglar coming away from a job and especially when that cop only has a few months of service and is only 19 years old.

In the bag was £331, in cash and a quantity of gold leaf. He had burgled his works, pinching the wages which he and his mates would have received the next day. He worked for a painting and decorators, thus the gold leaf. £331 is worth around £5000, as of 2020.

When the burglar appeared at court the chairman of the court said, 'The bench wished to commend the off duty officer for his alertness and apprehension of the man.' The chief constable endorsed the commendation. The day after the court case, the billboards of the local paper read, 'Young off duty PC traps £300 raider.'

AN ARREST IN DARLINGTON

Around about 1970, I was visiting my Mam in Darlington and I was happy to hear that she had met a nice man, Cliff Lloyd but everyone knew him as Pop. He was about the same age as Mam, 60'ish. They eventually married and were happy together, until sadly Mam died in her late 70s and a couple of years after, Pop also passed away. For the time being, they had not started to live together and only Mam and I were indoors and it was afternoon. Mam's house was still a council property and just at the bottom of the rear garden was the railway line, running from Darlington to Stockton. This was the very route on which the engine, The Locomotion No 1, had first carried fare-paying passengers in 1825. Now the main engines on that line were diesel.

We heard a knock on the front door and Mam answered it. It was a girl and a boy from next door. They were twins and were about 11. They enquired, "Mrs Curry is there a policeman here?" Mam said, "Yes." What they told of, was that a train had passed under the bridge, just up from Mam's house and some youths had thrown a stone off the bridge. It had smashed the windscreen of the passenger train. The driver was hurt and the train had stopped. I ran to the bridge and yes the train was stopped. The twins pointed to a group of youths and told me which one had thrown the stone. I collared him. The local police attended and I handed him over. I gave the names and address of the twins to the attending PC.

166

I was 20 and had made yet another good nick whilst off duty and 300 miles off my patch. I should have had another chief constable's commendation but I never heard another thing from the Darlington cop. The local cop had obviously not mentioned me, thus stealing the glory for himself. It had to be the case that he never mentioned me because he did not come back for a statement. So he would have had to word his statement something like this; 'I saw twins.......and as a result of what they told me, I saw a youth fitting their description, I spoke to him and he admitted to me that he had'......The PC must have been short of arrests, I never was.

Later, I was to discover that at least the twins received recognition for their actions. They also received a £50 British Rail reward. You will hear again of one of the twins, the girl, further on.

TRAINING CONTINUES

For the first 2 years of service of any police officer, he/she is on probation. That means if your frequent assessments throughout that period are not satisfactory then your service may be terminated and no other reason other than it is believed you are 'unlikely to become a good and efficient officer,' need be given. The 2 years probationary period can be a worry to some. However, it was not to cause me any worry or problems whatsoever. My practical policing proved to be well above average and I very soon developed a most acute coppers nose which is something that tells you that all is not quite right. You may not be sure what exactly it is but you instinctively know you are onto a wrong 'un. Not every cop is blessed with this gift but my results over the years suggest that I was.

After the initial course at Sandgate and for the next two years every fortnight, I and all probationers would have to attend a full day's probationer class at Chichester. The classes were more relaxed and the sergeant instructors more amenable to a bit of fun. As my reputation grew as a prolific thief-taker, I was comfortable to once again gradually take up my crown as 'class clown.' I like to think of myself as a wit rather than a clown but either way, now I would not be labelled, as I was in class 4a, as being a 'dimwit'. My practical police performance far contradicted that label, I believed.

One instructor sergeant, PS Mick Herbert, a lovely man, courted and married a WPC who was in my class and she became Lynne Herbert. Mick loved a joke and I obliged many times. I will tell of one such time when he was lecturing us on the Theft Act. He gave a set of circumstances and asked us to say what offence had been committed. This is what he said, "A vagrant goes to the door of a house and on his way along the path he sees many plastic gnomes in the garden. Believing the occupant would not know it was their own, he picked one up. He spoke to the occupant and he asked if they would like to purchase the said gnome. The occupant parted with the cash and he left. What offence has been committed?" Now I knew only too well that it was that of, criminal deception. This one was perfect for me and the PS said, " Tom?" I said, "I don't know what the offence is but I certainly know what the moral of the story is." Mick appeared to be fully prepared for a quip and said, "And that is?" I said, "There's no gnome like your own gnome."

I coasted through my 2 years probationary period and was officially appointed as a PC. That meant now I'd have to be given a bona fide reason for dismissal as opposed to the 2 years probationary very vague, 'not likely to make a good and efficient officer.'

MARRIAGE AND DIVORCE

In about 1970, a young policewoman was posted to Worthing her name was Angela. We began dating and we married about 1 year later. We were the same age, 22 years old. However, the marriage failed and we were divorced about 5 years later. It became apparent we wanted different things from life. I developed let's say a roving eye and I accept I was perhaps 75% at fault, for the failure of the marriage. Although it was planned, fortunately, we did not have a child together because we were then able to move on separately in life without any further contact. If there is a child you may not be able to do that because the child ensures there is a connection, even if that is only passed on information. There is no need to reference that part of my life again, other than to say I continue to wish Angela well.

ONLY A FLARE!

In the 70s, a large residential housing estate was built at Durrington, Worthing. During the excavations, what was thought to be a bomb was unearthed. The police were called and a young

PC attended. He viewed the suspected bomb and told the builders to keep away from it. He reported on his radio that he believed the army bomb disposal team should be called out. However, he was told that his sergeant, who had been in the army and said he had some expertise in such matters, would be with him shortly.

The sergeant arrived and inspected the item and stated that he had worked alongside the army disposal team and this suspected bomb was a harmless signal flare. He told the young PC that he had done the right thing, seeing as he did not know anything about such things. It was only about a foot long and with small fins and with that the sergeant picked it up by a fin and said, "We'll take it back to the nick." He put it in the passenger footwell of the police car and accompanied by the PC headed off for the nick, which was about 3 miles away in the town centre. On the way, whilst negotiating roundabouts, the flare was rocking about in the footwell.

At the nick was a large reinforced metal storage box, where such items deemed to be not dangerous and therefore not requiring urgent attention could be stored safely, to await the regular quarterly visits by the army disposal team. They would collect and take them away for disposal. This action meant that they did not have to be called out for relatively safe items, such as flares or gun ammunition etc. Surprisingly, the site of this box was within the confines of the nick, in an open square area surrounded by enclosed corridors on all 4 sides

The item from the building site was placed in the box on top of the sand that was inside. The box was locked again and then the
170

details were recorded in a book kept by the station sergeant and would be endorsed 'collected by bomb disposal,' as and when that was done.

The flare stayed in situ in the box and occasionally more small items were added as was the norm. Time passed and so came the day when the army team arrived for their regular collection. On opening the box the guy said, "Bloody hell. How did that get here?" He indicated to the alleged flare. He was told the story and he said, "That's no flare, it's a bomb and what's more it could go off at any time if you mess about with it. It will have to be disposed of right here." This was not what the station sergeant wanted to hear, taking into consideration the location of the box. Of course, the balloon went up then, with much group whispering, twitching and head-scratching amongst those who held rank.

No matter what other suggestions were made the experts were adamant that there was no other alternative available. It would have to be blown up right where it was and the sooner the better. So with no other option on the table arrangements had to be made to protect life and property from the pending blast. It took time to acquire the number of sandbags that were required and for windows in the surrounding corridors to be boarded up.

Many were reminded of the blitz and morale amongst those of rank was so low, I suggested we might request a visit from Vera Lynne but I was told to, "Shhhh!"

The hour cometh and the nick was evacuated and the bomb was detonated and it having been underestimated, considerable property damage still occurred to the nick. Worse than that was the expansive and expensive display windows, of Dutton Forshaw's Daimler showroom, next-door to the nick were shattered. The 'all clear' sounded and the big clear up commenced. It appeared to us that no action was taken against the sergeant and so we took our own and from then on nicknamed him, Pike, (You stupid boy!) from TV's Dad's Army.

FUN ON THE SECTION

One of our sergeants was a man I was very fond of but I did find him frustrating because he could never remember the names of anyone or anything and got around it by referring to items as doinses and whatsisnames etc.

He also cursed a lot which may have been for the reason that it gave him more time to think of the name. He was a lovely man with a heart of gold and it was just his way, no malice whatsoever and in fact, we were friends. I always called him sarge at work but we were on Christian name terms. He was a big man and had a deep voice. One day he spoke to me in his office and it went something like this; "Here, I say whatname, urr, urr." I said, "Tom, sarge." He said," I know your f.......g name, wise guy. I can't forget you. You wanna learn to wait and give people a chance." I said, "Sorry sarge." He said, "Before I finish what I was going to tell you, put yer moniker on this billy-doo" and he handed me a G30, a police report form. I signed it and gave it back to him and he said, "What was I saying?" I said, "I don't know, sarge" to which he said, "Will you shut the f... up a minute and let me think." I

172

thought I better keep quiet, no matter how long he takes. He paused, "Oh! Yeah, that was it. I'll tell ya what I bought the other day, a new whatamacallit. I got it at that whatsits place up on the thingabee estate near old doinses place, What's his blinkin name again? He used to be married to old whatsisnames daughter. I'll tell you where he used to be, up by what's the bloody name of the place again? Opposite, thingybobs." I said, "Sarge just tell me what you bought."He said, "For f...sake Pete, Harry urr, will you ever learn to stop interrupting people and give em a chance. I was telling you, a shed a new garden shed, I bought." He really was sometimes every bit as bad as that. I miss him because he passed away. He's gone to whatsisname in the sky!

During the same period, we had on our section a young probationer who thought he knew it all and he always appeared to be over-enthusiastic to impress. We'll call him, George.

At an early turn briefing, the sarge says, "Old doins is off today sick and somebody has to do his lollypop duty." George says, "That's on my beat sarge, so I'll cover that." Sarge says, "The times are..." George says, "I've got the times, sarge." "Righto wise guy, get on with it then," says the sarge. Anyway, I'm single crewed in a marked car and the sarge comes out with me and around lunchtime, he says to me, "Take me to em, what's the name of the road and we'll see how old thingybob's getting on with he's whatname." So by now, I can interpret what the sarge says and so I head for Ham Road to check how George is getting on with his fill-in school crossing duty. Well, when we get there I cannot believe what I'm seeing because George is out in the middle of the road sure enough but you'll never guess what? He ain't wearing a police uniform. He has on a black beret, white coat and is holding a school crossing sign. Well at first I laughed but then thinking he was a cop the same as me I began to cringe. The sarge says, "What the f...s going on here for f...sake."

 The sarge gets out and I think I'll hide in the glove compartment but then I get out of the car because I might miss something. So whilst trying to curtail my mirth, I toddle along behind the sarge. George is still out in the middle of the road holding up the traffic with the lollypop stick. Sarge goes to the edge of the kerb and shouts, "Here, whatsit a word." George says, "Just a minute sarge." Sarge says, "Never mind just a minute, get over here, now!" George comes over and sarge says, "What's with the f...ing gear?" George says, "At first I was out there with my police uniform on and then Harry from the greengrocers asked where Cyril was. I told him he's off sick and I'm here to do his job today. Harry said Cyril leaves his gear in my shop, so you can have it if you want and so I changed and put it on." Sarge says, "You're a f...ing policeman, you idiot. You don't need that f...ing gear!" George pleaded, "But sarge, you told me I was to do his lollypop duty." Sarge said, "You better get that f...ing gear off before I really lose my rag!" George thought he was hard done by and I thought, I never want to be a sergeant. I promise you, that story is without a word of a lie.

WHO INTERVIEWS THESE GUYS?

Far too frequently you would come across guys who should never have been accepted into the police and I'd think who the hell is interviewing these fellers? I could tell in an instant that they were not up to the job and one such guy was a young Welshman and so let's call him Di. He was short, small build and so the first thing I thought was who measured him because he cannot be 5'8". Then I thought, maybe the doctor who did my medical is still alive and now as well as his hearing and chest packing up, now his eyesight has failed him too!

One of our section had been promoted to sergeant, Mick Hogan, a lovely genuine guy and he was leaving us. I was tasked with organising a whip-round for the usual tankard. We were on nights and I said to Di, "You haven't been with us that long but do you want to chip in 50p. too?" Di said, "I'd like to put in but can I give you it tomorrow night because I don't carry money on me when I'm on nights in case I'm mugged?" I said, "Are you winding me up?"He said, "No, I am serious." I said, "Do you have your truncheon on you?" He said, "Yes I do." I said, "You're a policeman man. If anyone tries to mug you part their f.....g hair with that and they won't try and mug you again." He just said, "Thank you. I'll remember that." He was always very polite.

Another time the same guy did a witness statement and the sergeant said, "What's this you've put here?" He said, "Ah! Yes, sergeant, I wasn't sure if I needed to put that in and I asked another PC and he said I should." The sergeant said, "Look it is not right and you should not be asking other PC's stuff because you need to get things right. If you want to know anything whatsoever you just come to me, that's what I am here for. Come to me, got it?" He said, "Yes sergeant I will do that." So a few days went by and we're on the night shift again. The sergeant was in the station sergeant's office and the phones were going, the hotline was going, burglar alarms were going off, the radios were going and then Di comes into the office passing other PC's in the corridor on the way. He goes straight to the sergeant and says, "Can I ask you a question, sergeant?" The sergeant must have thought, he's getting the hang of it now. I'm busy but I did tell him to come to me and he stopped what he was doing and said, "Yes of course Di, what is it?" Di said, "Can you tell me please sergeant, where is the light switch to put the lights on in the hall?" The sergeant said, "For f...sake Di, you can ask another PC that!" I kid you not, hopeless!

He was told he had to go and guard a house which was a murder scene. We were on nights and it was winter and he was told you can take your own car and sit in it because you will be there until morning apart for ¾ an hour when you will be relieved for your meal break. He had his break and the sergeant thought he'd go and check that he was ok at about 2 am. He was more than ok. He was asleep in a sleeping bag on the back seat of his car with an alarm clock next to him, set for 5.30 am.

One time we went to an intruder alarm ringing at a club. We were told the keyholder would not be with us for an hour or more. A window was open but I thought in error. I said to Di, "You're the smallest get through that window and see if you can open the door so we can check the place. We can't wait here for an hour when it looks ok." He said, "No I'm not doing that there might be somebody in there." I said, "Get in there!"

Di was on the enquiry desk one time and he had to report a driver for a traffic offence. He went to the sergeant and said, "Sarge, I'm reporting someone for a traffic accident and he's trying to be funny with me. I've asked him for his occupation and he says he is a nun but he's a man. Can you have a word with him?" The sergeant said, "Nun, you mean a monk don't you?" He said, "No, he definitely says he's a nun." The sergeant said, "Ok I'll be there in a minute." The sergeant went to the man and said, "Right sir, what is your occupation?" He replied, "Nun, err...... I haven't got one. I'm unemployed."

Some of these people do eventually get weeded out but I have known many who have been carried for their full thirty years.

A COOL DUDE BURGLAR

I am going to tell you about the coolest guy I ever nicked. I'd been at Worthing a few years when we had a tip-off that a Working Men's Club was going to be burgled. So a new probationer and I got into our jeans, T-shirts and anoraks. After the club closed we were inside in the dark, sat down to await our guy's arrival. At about 2 am, we saw a shadow pass a rear window and then heard the smashing of glass and then someone running away. My mate moved and I whispered, "I reckon he'll be back. He's run-off and will be watching to see if any alarm goes off or the cops arrive."

Low and behold, that's what happened. Suddenly the shadow was there again. I can reveal to you that no matter how often you do this as a cop, at this stage your heart is pounding so loud you think the suspect will hear it. You're not frightened but it's just adrenaline kicking in. So then without any sound, except for the wall clock ticking, a gloved hand comes through the broken window and pushes the handle up to open it. A shadowy figure climbs in and walks silently to the bar area. We can see him but we are in the darkest corner. I know he has to go behind the bar to get to any goodies. So I have positioned us so that once he's on the other side of the bar counter, we have him trapped and I will hit the light switch.

The figure fumbles inside his coat and then a jemmy (crowbar) is in his hand. He puts it under the bar shutter and it cracks open. He climbs over the counter, now he's behind the bar and we have him trapped. I hit the light switch and the light goes on. Our guy does not look up or around. He just casually leans on the bar and says in a calm voice, "What are you having then lads?" He was as easy to deal with as could be and I can say, almost a pleasure. I liked him but we nicked him all the same.

WHY DID THE POLICE NOT THINK OF THAT?

I recall another time when I had a prisoner for theft. He said to me, "Can I ask you a question?" I said "Yes." He said, "You know when the police show a photo of a bloke and say he is wanted for questioning?" I said, "Yes." He said, "Well, why didn't they

question him when they took his photo?" I said," Are you
serious?" I could see he was and he replied, "Yeah."

AIR CRASH AT SOUTHDOWN GLIDING CLUB

I want to tell you now of an incident that really shook me. My
brother Alan, who I mentioned earlier on, had moved to
Basingstoke but still commuted every weekend to The Southdown
Gliding Club but it had also moved from Firle Beacon in East Sussex
to Storrington in West Sussex, just outside of Worthing. Worthing
Police did not cover Storrington and there was a small sub-station
there that did. The duties of the Storrington guys often brought
them to our neck of the woods. Alan was then a qualified
instructor and as such would take his turn at being weekend duty
instructor. The club by now, instead of using a mechanical winch
had a Chipmunk single-engine aircraft. As Alan was one of the few
members who also held a power pilots licence, he would be flying
the tow plane all this particular weekend and I knew this.

We were on the late shift and at about 4 pm, I saw a Storrington
officer who I knew. For no particular reason and most likely just to
make polite conversation, I said, "What are you up to then?" or
something along those lines. He said, "The Chipmunk at the gliding
club has crashed and the instructor has been killed." I nearly
collapsed because it just had to be Alan after all he was the only
instructor on duty there. I said, "What's his name?" He gave me a
name that was not Alan. I only realised later that the PC knew I
was PC Tom Curry and he would probably have put two and two

together and would have known I was related if it had been Alan Curry. How then did it come about that it was not Alan?

It was a Sunday and Alan had been towing with the Chipmunk all weekend. Now the vast majority of members live for flying and cannot keep away from the place. What happened was another instructor, who was not on duty, had a run-out with his wife and of course, ended up at the club. Itching to get into the air, he said to Alan, "I'll give you a break and do a couple of tows for you." Alan got out of the cockpit and he climbed in and took off. The engine stalled and it plummeted to earth and the poor man was fatally injured.

I MEET A CHAMPION JOCKEY

One day in 1974, I went to a house on the seafront in Worthing. My purpose for the visit was to interview a female who had been involved in a road traffic accident. Whilst I was there a small young man was present and sat quietly throughout. The interview concluded and I recall a conversation with the young man, which began with him saying, "You guys are not keen on jockeys." He went on to say that he had been stopped by the police whilst driving many times, getting to and fro on race days.

I said to him, "Are you a jockey then?" He said, "Yes, I'm Pat Eddery. Have you heard of me?" I said, "No, I haven't but I'm Tom Curry and I don't expect you've heard of me either." We both laughed and it appeared to break down any barrier there might have been between us and we then engaged in a very pleasant conversation. I explained that I did not follow horse racing but I

180

was on duty at Goodwood Races in a few weeks. Pat said that he was riding at that meeting and went on to say the following, "I have enjoyed the chat and I don't normally do this but I'll give you a tip. I'm riding a horse called Spring Step and it is going to win." We shook hands and I left.

On the day of the races, I was there in full uniform and I had not thought anymore about the tip I was given. Whenever we were on duty at the races, we'd be reminded to be aware of the TV cameras and that they might be on us, throughout the day.

I was standing by the fence at the parade ring when I saw Pat mounted and he spotted me. He gave me a thumbs up and with an index finger pointed down at the horse he was on. I gave a slight nod. I quickly checked and sure enough, the horse was the Spring Step. I spotted a plainclothes detective friend and asked him to place a bet for me on the horse. The price showing was 16/1. I gave him £1 and he said that he personally would give me better odds as the horse was an outsider and stood no chance. Nevertheless, I told him to place the bet. Pat and Spring Step won the race easily. In today's money, I had gambled £10.49p. and I had won a very nice return of £167.85p. I put a £1 on Lester Piggott's horse in the next race and he won at 4/1. So I had a very lucrative day out.

I started to take an interest in horse racing from then on. I must say, I was slightly embarrassed to learn that charming Pat Eddery, was Champion jockey for the first time, of his 11 occasions, that year, 1974. Pat was to become one of the greatest jockeys of all time. Sadly, he passed away at the age of 63 in 2015. He was 3 years younger than me. It is a pity that I never got the opportunity to remind Pat of our meeting as young men, both starting in our chosen careers.

A HIGH SPEED STOLEN CAR CHASE WITH A DANGEROUS ESCAPEE FROM HMP

In 1974, I was again commended by the chief constable for my 'high degree of attention to duty and high-speed chase in pursuit of a potentially dangerous criminal, who had escaped from HMP Canterbury,' where he was serving time for shooting a cop.

During the early hours of the morning, I was single manned in a marked police car, a Hillman Avenger. I saw a Triumph 2000 a better car than I was in, coming towards me and I thought he was a bit slow dipping the headlights. I turned my car around and thought I would follow him for a bit and see if he made any further errors. However, he took off and I chased it in circles around the town at speeds of up to 60 miles an hour and through red traffic lights and he was driving like a maniac. I was alone in the car and as well as drive, I had to keep up a commentary on the radio to guide in other officers.

He eventually drove into a dead-end and bailed out of the car and disappeared into the dark. I gave chase but lost him in some allotments. However, I caught up with a female, who had been in the stolen car and nicked her. In consideration of how potentially dangerous he might be and that he was a prison escapee, roadblocks were set up sealing off the town as best we could. They remained in place for about the next 6 hours or so.

At about 8 am he was arrested as he sat in the back of a taxi, about 3 miles from where he decamped from the Triumph 2000. A big man of about 18 stones, this time he was unarmed and outnumbered. He gave up without a fight. None of us were armed back then, no firearms trained officers were called and neither was there a helicopter available. If there had been as now, I believe the heat-seeking device would have lead us to him in the allotments or nearby because no one else was about at that hour.

ANOTHER CHASE WITH ARMED ROBBERS

During the 70s, one Saturday at about 3 pm, I recall I was double crewed with another PC on motor patrol. I was driving and a radio message was broadcast that there had been an armed robbery at a jeweller's shop in Warwick Street. A shotgun had been fired into the ceiling. The gang had made off in a Ford Capri. We were right on the spot and there in front of us heading towards Brighton, was the car and we put out a message.

It must have seen us and it took off with us in pursuit. The traffic was heavy. There were 3 or four inside the car. It turned into what we knew was a cul-de-sac. We chased after it and we were joined by a sergeant in another car. At the bottom, it turned around and came back towards us. A shotgun was poking out the window, it fired. The sergeant's car ran across the pavement and smashed into a brick wall. He was now out of it.

The Capri turned and headed back towards the town once more, with us chasing. It was on the wrong side of the road, on a bend, then it went through red traffic lights and rocketed away.

Someone could get killed! I did the right thing, even though I did not want to and I stopped. They were never caught, for that job anyway but my guess is another time and place, they were. If now was then, they would not have gotten away, with a police helicopter tracking them.

I BECOME A FIREARMS OFFICER

I thought the next time a gun is pointed in my direction I'd like to be on an equal footing. So shortly after the robbery incident, I applied for a firearms course. I qualified as a marksman with a Walther PP (police pistol) 9mm, the one James Bond carried but the difference was Bond was fictional. He was acting but I was not. My new toys were to be fast cars and now guns. On the Sterling submachine gun, I qualified as an expert marksman. The police sterling was not a machine gun as such but a single shot (for police use) firearm.

FIREARMS DUTY AT GATWICK AIRPORT

I was one of the first Sussex police full-time armed officers, at Gatwick Airport, in the early 70s but I was still based at Worthing but seconded for months. In my time, my gun was not on view and I wore no body armour and the small Walther fitted into my trouser pocket out of sight. We were to tell no one we were armed. We worked in pairs and the same shifts as at Worthing.

When the jumbo jets landed, suddenly scores of American tourists would spot us, in full uniform with helmets and they would swamp us. They called out, "There's a Bobby. Hi, Bobby. Do they still call
184

you guys, Bobbies?" I thought no, they call us, the filth, pigs, bastards etc. but I just said, "Yes." We were asked to pose for photos, being asked, "Can you put your arm around my wife, Bobby?" and autographs too. Q. "Can I have your autograph Bobby?" R. "No, sorry sir, we do photographs on Mondays, Wednesdays and Fridays and the other days are autograph days. Today is a Monday, so no autographs today, I'm afraid." R. "Oh! That's a shame. Honey, what day are we flying out?"

One typically dressed Yank, in a red blazer with a veterans badge, Rupert Bear type trousers, baseball cap and a camera around his neck bigger than a BBC TV outside broadcast camera, said to me, "Of course you guys still don't carry guns do you, Bobby?" R. "It looks like rain." He said, "Gee you sure have a fine country. I was over here during the war you know but my you look so young Bobby, you won't remember the war, will you, Bobby?" I said, "Yes, I do. That's the one Audie Murphy won." He yelled out, "Hey everybody, the Bobby's telling jokes." For those who do not know, Audie Murphy was the US most decorated soldier of WW2. After the war, he became an actor playing himself, in many allegedly true accounts of his exploits.

One piece of firearms training I enjoyed, was the quick draw and all the practise was done with live ammunition. The Walther would be put into a leather belt holster. You would be stood in front of 3 torso size targets, with a red light and a white light above each. If a white light went on you did nothing, if a red light went on you drew and fired. So it could be any one of 6 lights that illuminated. The targets were wired to a clock and the clock started when the light went on and stopped when the round hit the target.

You might be surprised to learn that I achieved a consistent point 9 of a second, occasionally less. Those of us there would have a shoot-off and the slowest got the teas, I never did pay. A well known and likeable PC stationed at Brighton, Jack Snipe, had his own fancy leather holster made. He hated that he could never beat me. He gave me the nickname of Kid Curry. I like to think it was after the TV cowboy character but it could have just been because I was so young. Anyway, I nicknamed him and put an R on the end of his surname, he became Jack Snipe..r! Anyway, it was fun.

I recall at Gatwick Airport on one occasion, when my partner PC Dave Perrin, a great friend of mine and I were overseeing an arrival flight from Belfast. As we stood together, a man came towards us with his hand in his jacket pocket, as if he had a gun. Luckily for him, he quickly took his hand out to reveal he was holding nothing. I say that because I was on the verge of drawing my Walther and Dave said he was too. The guy, of course, had no idea that we were armed. He apologised profusely and was visibly shaken when we took him to one side and in no uncertain terms told him how stupid his actions were and how close to death he had most likely come, i.e. probably as close as, point 9 of a second.

For short periods, I was bodyguard to the Duke of Norfolk inside Arundel Castle and Jim Callaghan PM at his Sussex farm and there were others too.

COINCIDENTAL NAMES

Mentioning Jack Snipe...r, has reminded me of the names of others I worked with. When I did a stint on CID at Worthing, there was one guy, Mick Reis and I always tried to avoid working with him. It was not because I didn't like him but I just did not want his name linked with mine, in any reporting in the papers. It had already been reported that police were called to The Curry House Restaurant to a disturbance and the PC who attended was PC...... Curry! I did not want them going further with Curry and Reis. (Reis, is German for rice and is pronounced in English, as rice.)

Tom and Gerry.

It went from bad to worse when at Worthing, I was teamed up on a car with PC Hall that was....Gerry (G not J) Hall.

Along the coast at Bognor Regis was a PC Tim Salt and at Chichester was a WPC Jackie Pepper.

Years later, a custody sergeant called John Pepper and I disagreed. The inspector spoke to me about it and I said, "If you mix Curry and Pepper together, things are bound to get heated!"

MATT WILSON AND THE MURDER/ROBBERY AT LLOYD'S BANK DURRINGTON, WORTHING, 1960

I said earlier that I would mention Matt Wilson again. My brother had lodged with Matt and his wife when he moved to Worthing. Matt had been a local taxi driver in Worthing but in the mid 70's he started work at Worthing Police Station as a driver orderly. His duties involved odd jobs but mainly driving the prison van to transport prisoners daily to various HMP's mainly in London. Of course, there had to be police escort and because I liked Matt's company, I would volunteer all the time to do that job and so together we did escorts to all the major HMP's.

I recall one time, going into the prison officer's mess at Pentonville and being served tea by prisoner trustees. Now although I may have looked young to many of the older prison officers, I had fast become experienced because of my mostly self generated workload. I had come in contact with murderers, armed robbers, been stabbed and assaulted countless times and commended on more than one occasion and so I was a bit put out when an arrogant officer said to me, in front of Matt and several other prison officers, "Come to see some real criminals have you lad?" I was reminded that we had been served by a trustee but now he was not within earshot and I found myself saying, "No, I don't need to because I'm out on the streets, where they are not tame!" I have to say, this proved to be a one-off and most times cops and screws got on well.

Incidentally, prison officers got the name screws because in the days when a convict was sentenced to hard labour if there was no work the inmates had to turn a handle on a revolving drum, which had no purpose other than to work and occupy the inmate. The officer had a screwdriver and could slacken or tighten a screw, to make it harder or easier to turn the handle and so they became known as screws.

You will read later, how in the 80s when the UK HMP's were at a bursting point, I became a gaoler overseeing remand prisoners temporarily housed in police cells.

Matt Wilson was a broad Scot and a lovely decent man. On the morning of 10 November 1960, he was working as a taxi driver in Worthing from the central British Rail station taxi rank. He was called to pick up 2 guys from Durrington, Worthing, about 2 or 3 miles away. He picked them up and he dropped them off on the seafront, near the town centre. He was pleasantly surprised when for a two and sixpenny fare, he was given a ten-shilling note and told to keep the change. (10 shillings in 1960 is equal to £11.60p. in 2020.) Cheered by the generosity he returned to the taxi rank. When he got back his mates at the rank told him that there had been an armed robbery at Lloyds bank in Durrington. It did not take long for the astute Matt to work out his hefty tip was very likely from those connected with the robbery.

Matt headed hotfoot to the nick and a detective sergeant jumped in the taxi with Matt and they went to the seafront. Matt saw the two and pointed them out to the DS and the 2 men were nicked without any trouble. It was a brilliant bit of work by the public-spirited Matt who then returned to the taxi rank.

Earlier at Lloyds Bank, a London man called Victor John Terry, his girlfriend and the 2 arrested men entered the building. A 61-year-old guard John Pull was shot at close range with a shotgun and killed by Terry. They fled with £1,372 (Worth £26,473 in 2020). Later, following a tip-off from a landlady in Scotland, Terry and his girlfriend were also captured.

On 25 May 1961, Terry was hanged. The other 2 were, Alan Hosier aged 20 and 16-year-old Philip Tucker. Hosier was given a life sentence and Tucker, who was under 18, was ordered to be detained during Her Majesty's Pleasure. Valerie Salter aged 18 years and the girlfriend of Terry, was given 1 year's probation order.

An interesting fact is that on the way to commit the robbery and murder, Terry heard on the car radio that his friend Francis Forsyth, aged 18 years, had just been hanged that very morning at Wandsworth Prison. Knowing this Terry was not deterred and still carried out the crime, for which he would also be subsequently hanged. Terry was to hang from the same gallows as Forsyth a little over 6 months later.

Lloyds Bank paid out £10,000 in reward money. (Worth approx. £195,000 in 2021.) Matt shared it with the Scottish landlady and one other person. His share paid off his house mortgage and he was able to buy his own taxi.

In 1994, when Matt sadly died, Lloyds Bank sent flowers.

INJURED WHILST EVICTING SQUATTERS

Whilst evicting squatters from a big house in Grand Avenue, I was stabbed in the side of my head as we broke the door down. A youth inside with a 6-foot length of copper piping, sharpened at one end, jabbed it out at me through a gap in the door. I saw it at the last second and turned my head as fast as I could and it struck me just in front of my left ear. A lucky break I thought, I could have lost an eye. It was quite a nasty injury and was stitched. The squatters smashed their way through onto the roof and a stand-off took place. I refused to leave the scene to go to the hospital until they came down and were arrested. My attacker went to prison for 2 years, a period much more than the others.

2 MORE INJURIES WITH MY JINX

During this period, on 2 separate occasions, whilst attending disturbances, I sustained quite serious back injuries, requiring hospitalisation. Those responsible were arrested and appeared in court. A PC who battled alongside me, Dave Stamp, later promoted to sergeant, was with me on each occasion. Dave is a thoroughly decent and reliable man. Although we are very different in character, we are still firm friends, even though I often refer to him as my jinx! I continue to enjoy the company of Dave and his lovely wife, Caryl.

ARREST OF MALES FOR GROSS INDECENCY OFFENCES

Throughout the 70s, I frequently worked with many other PC's, in jeans and T-shirts, passing on my knowledge of the offences I am about to mention, as it was to me, by a very fine man, retired Chief Inspector John Ranger. I was tasked with the detection and apprehension of males who frequented local gent's toilets and committed various sexual gross indecency offences. I, over the years, developed a unique expertise in their detection and I caught all the offenders in the act. It is difficult to say how many I was instrumental in putting before the courts but it is certainly in 3 figures. The males were from most walks of life and I would guess 90% were not true homosexuals and were without any outward mannerisms or characteristics sometimes attributed. I guess well over half were married men.

Throughout the remainder of my career, I continued to make arrests of males committing gross indecency offences in public toilets, whether I was in uniform or not but the former does involve a greater degree of stealth.

OFFENDER HAD BEEN A HUGE, CHILD FILM STAR

I will tell of one such occasion when I was in uniform at the beginning of 1976. I am only willing to divulge scant details. The time was getting on for 11 pm and it was dark. I saw a car parked near a male toilet, which I knew was a location where frequent offences took place. I approached the car from the rear and shone my torch inside. I saw two males, both adults, indulging in an act of gross indecency, which is strictly forbidden in a public place.

The owner/driver of the car had been a huge, child film star and although older then, he was still recognisable. In all sexual offence cases, corroboration is required and as one of the offenders was under 21 years, the consent of the Director of Public Prosecutions had to be sought at that time, prior to charging. If one or both men admit the offence then that would be deemed to be corroboration.

I had dealt with many such cases, involving an under 21year old. I was fully aware that previous consent requests from the DPP to prosecute had not been granted, in preference to an official police caution being given. I decided that to arrest on this occasion, would be a waste of public money and also my time. I also thought that strong words from me probably would have exactly the same desired effect, as visiting a uniformed inspector for him to offer his advice. I was not one to mince my words on such occasions and I let them know in no uncertain terms, that if I caught them again I'd be feeling their collars.

Up to 1967, homosexuality was against the law, full stop. In 1967 the law was changed to allow over 21's to indulge but with certain restrictions. In 1994 the age of consent was lowered to 18 years. 6 years later in 2000, the age was lowered again and this time to 16 years. My own opinion is the age should have remained at 18 years. I feel that many young men at 16 years old may not have matured sufficiently, to make the right lifetime decision and thus may be susceptible to persuasion/corruption.

I have no problem with anyone's sexuality but such acts should be confined to privacy and not take place in a public toilet, a place where decent people frequent for a legitimate bodily function. I am not going to go into any further detail about other offences of a similar nature. I felt the need to make some mention because of the long periods which I spent dealing with such matters in the 70s.

AIDE TO CID

In the 70s I did my first 3 months as an aide to CID and after which, I was offered a permanent position as a detective but not at Worthing because my wife of the time was a WDC in the department. I was offered a post at Chichester 20 miles away. I explained that we were only newly married and could not afford a second car. The detective chief inspector knew my wife because she was part of his team. He said to me, "What about a motorbike?" I said, "My wife can't ride a motorbike." He either did not get my quip or he didn't reckon it. He said, "I meant for you." Anyway, I turned it down and never regretted it.

Shortly after, I went back to the CID because there had been a double murder in the town. An elderly couple, their surname being Gales, were murdered with a hammer. The offender was their son and the motive was to gain his early inheritance. Most of the local detectives were put on the murder enquiry. Left to deal with the daily routine CID work, were 2 regular DC's and one detective sergeant, Bernie Wells. Normally, to man the CID office, there was a detective inspector, 4 detective sergeants and about

15 detective constables. Now there was one DS, two regular DC's and me, an aide. The 2 DC's paired up and Bernie and I became partners. I was about 26 and Bernie was 13 years older. Additionally, poor Bernie was left to do the work of the DI, and 4 DS's. I always have said, the hard bit for him was being my partner!

Everything worked out very well and we held the fort for weeks until the others came back. We worked longer hours than the murder squad. They received a chief constable's commendation and we 4 covering and well undermanned, got no recognition whatsoever.

Considering our age difference and police experience, Bernie and I got along great and we are still very good friends, nearly 45 years later. I learnt a lot from Bernie, who retired as a superintendent. He oversaw many high profile cases. He was in charge of the Babes in the Wood double child murder at Brighton, the first time around, when the jury acquitted Russell Bishop. Bernie knew all along it was him but forensics was not as they are now. Bishop faced trial again 30+ years later and thankfully he was convicted. Bernie was also second in command of the Brighton Bombing. He was a great detective and a lovely man. I'm proud to still be his friend.

A TEAM COMMENDATION

In 1978 I was part of a 4 man operational squad, who worked in casual clothes, T-shirts jeans etc. It was formed to combat increased crime in Worthing and during a period spanning only a few months, the team arrested and charged 135 persons for a variety of criminal offences, including burglaries and thefts. The chairmen of the local court commended the team for the arrests and how we prepared the cases against 27 young persons for 54 criminal offences. The chief constable endorsed the commendation.

FATAL ROAD TRAFFIC ACCIDENT

I attended many fatal accidents but I just want to briefly mention one of them. One day during the late 1970s, I was sent to an accident in Durrington Lane. When I got there, I saw an Austin Westminster car on its roof and an elderly male passenger inside was dead. A Triumph Herald, a lightly built car, had failed to stop at the stop sign at the crossroads and had clipped the edge of the rear nearside of the big heavy Austin and flipped it over. I formed the opinion that was only possible because the lighter car had struck the very edge of the Austin. I reckon if it had collided full side on, it would not have had the weight to flip it over. The drivers of both cars were unhurt. The driver of the Austin was known to me, it was off duty Inspector Eric Hollin, the very man who had been so instrumental in my appointment. The deceased I recall was his father in law. It seemed ironic that I would be the first cop on the scene and would support him at such a sad time, almost as a thank you, I thought.

LICENSED TO SPY

In the early 80s, I did several initial 'spy' jobs in licensed premises, which were suspected of breaching the regulations of their drinks licence and/or drug dealing. These premises were mainly late night drinking establishments. One was a nightclub in Bognor Regis and the licence had expired. They were suspected of continuing to operate without a late-night drinks licence. The membership was strictly for known members and their guests and so no one outside of that had actually been inside the building and witnessed alcohol being served. It may seem obvious that a breach of the licensing laws was taking place from the late-night comings and goings. However, the local police licensing officer was not prepared to commit to any police raid, without first making absolutely certain evidentially, that alcohol was being served.

Although two other attempts were made by officers to gain undercover entry, they both had failed. Subsequently, I was asked to give it a try. I chose a policewoman to accompany me and her name was Jo. We dressed in smart plain clothes and prepared to gain entry. We had a pre-drink in a pub and those days, I smoked socially. The brand of cigarettes I smoked was Dunhill, which had a red packet with gold paper inner wrapping and a white tissue backing. I tore small pieces of all the different coloured papers and added some blue paper from a paper towel. I sprinkled a small amount of the papers into the hair of my female colleague and just a tiny amount in my own.

We pushed the entry buzzer at the club and a doorman answered it. He asked if we were members and I said. "No." He said, "Sorry but it is strictly a members club and their guests. Wait a minute, are you a honeymoon couple?" I said, "What makes you say that?" He said, "Confetti in your hair." I brushed my hair with my hand and my colleagues. He said, "Hang on I'll get someone to sign you in." We were duly signed in as Mr and Mrs Connor by a stranger and were admitted into the club. I bought drinks to prove the sale, music was being played and we had a dance. At one stage the management announced there was a honeymoon couple present and we received a round of applause and the offer of a complimentary drink.

After a very pleasant evening, we left the club with the evidence requested, a description of the staff present and a plan in my head of the layout of the premises, if needed for a later police raid. However, it was never the subject of a raid, as it was decided to close the club down and no licence was ever applied for again. So it was a successful conclusion. I was spared having to give evidence at court and of being recognised as the newly married, Mr Connor, who had 'conned' his way in. I simply could not resist the name!

Lovely Jo and I were both single and had enjoyed the evening so much, we continued to date for some time after.

COMMENDED FOR BRAVERY

On the 11th August 1982, I was single crewed in a marked police car, when I was sent to a man going berserk during a domestic dispute. On the way and on seeing a young probationer, PC Gary Tutt, I took it upon myself to pick him up and take him along. When we got to the address, we found that a man had smashed his mother's lovely home to pieces. She had run from the house to escape his violent attack. Gary and I went to the front door and it was immediately thrown open. The man rushed at us, pointing a loaded, high-powered by gas, diver's speargun.

There was little time but I managed to jump aside and grab the speargun, whilst endeavouring to keep it pointed away from us, as we struggled violently to contain him. The man still holding the speargun, grabbed Gary's somewhat heavy personal radio from its harness and smashed him over the head with it. Gary was knocked unconscious and collapsed. I continued to struggle with the man on the ground and during this time, I spotted the leather strap of Gary's truncheon sticking out from his pocket. I grabbed it and heaved it out, all the time holding on to the speargun and struggling with the man. In a split second, I had the truncheon and I belted him with it, straight on the top of his head as hard as I could. I had now knocked him out. Gary came around and we cuffed the man behind his back. We searched him and found he had two lethal-looking diving daggers hidden on him. One was tucked in the belt of his trousers and the other was strapped to his lower leg. The man was gushing blood and we were all covered.

After he came around, we took him to the car and bandaged his head to try and stem the blood. Other officers arrived and we were happy to hand him over, whilst Gary and I recovered. The man who was covered in blood had not said anything up to now but I will never forget what he did say. He looked straight at me and said and I promise this is word for word exactly, "I'll tell you what, you've ruined my day." Phew! I'll tell you what too, he got very close to ruining ours!

His mother was extremely grateful to us. The man needed stitches. Gary had a bump the size of an egg on his head but no stitches were required.

Our section inspector, John Albon, did a report to the chief constable recommending both of us to be honoured with a Queen's Police Medal. John's direct boss Superintendent A, we'll call him, endorsed the report that he did not agree and poor John was told he should not have made the recommendation. Without Superintendent A's endorsement, the QPM award was not going to happen and it did not. Superintendent A had shown some signs that he disliked me. Further on you will read more and to what extent. Inspector Albon went on to become a deputy chief constable thus overtaking the rank of Superintendent A.

We were given a chief constable's commendation, for the 'courage and tenacity we displayed in disarming and arresting the disturbed man, who was subsequently not charged with any offence but was committed to a psychiatric hospital'.

Gary a fresh probationer had received his baptism and he too now had a chief constable's commendation, in his first few months of police service, as I had. He proved to be a good copper and did his full 30 years and retired with the rank of detective sergeant.

A year or two later, the man and his mother came to the nick and asked to see us. Gary was not available but I saw them. The man had now fully recovered and had been released from the psychiatric hospital. He said he wanted to say sorry to us. He was a good and decent man and I told him so, before shaking his hand. As far as is I know, he did not come to the police notice again.

MY RELATIONSHIP WITH THE DIVISIONAL COMMANDER HITS ROCK BOTTOM

I now move to a part of my life that was not enjoyable and I don't even like to look back on it. I mentioned Superintendent A and I said that he did not like me. Well, that would certainly prove to be the case. Up to a certain point, there had been no problem between us and he never had any cause whatsoever to criticise my work.

I believe things really started to deteriorate at the time of retired Sergeant Joe Rowland's death, who I also mentioned earlier. Joe retired and sadly a few years later he died, in 1982. We had kept in contact and I visited him frequently. When Joe died, his son, Brian, came to see me. He said Joe's widow and all the family, wished for the coffin to be draped with the Sussex police flag, for the 6 pall-bearers to be close friends, all serving officers and in uniform. This sort of send-off is normally for officers who die in service but it is not strictly reserved for such an occasion. In other words, if either the deceased himself or the widow wants it, there is no reason why it should not be done. Brian said that his Mum had asked if I could arrange it. I said I would have to speak to Superintendent A and I would get back to him.

I was shocked when I saw the superintendent because he was thoroughly obnoxious. There is little point in going into it with any detail but he said, "He's not entitled to it." I said that I had checked it out and it was as aforementioned. He said he did not want anything to do with it and I would have to contact HQ. I did just that and HQ said if the widow wants it, then go ahead.

I told Brian I would arrange it but nothing about what the superintendent had said. I got 6 pall-bearers, including me and I thought it would be good, with 2 inspectors at the front, 2 sergeants in the middle and 2 PC's at the back, me being one of them. We had a practice run and that was about it, except I had to get the flag. I was told the superintendent had that in his office. I went to him and asked if I could have the flag, all very respectful, saying please and lots of sir's. He threw the flag at me and said, "Do not involve me!"

 So come the day of the funeral, there was as expected, an exceptional turnout because Joe was extremely well known and popular. Everything went to plan but I was surprised to see the hypocrite, Superintendent A, in attendance with his immediate boss the chief superintendent and both were in full uniform.

202

When it was all over, I thought it best to take a low profile and I waited until the superintendent was not around and I returned the flag, leaving it in his office.

All went quiet for a while and I made sure to keep out of the superintendent's way. However, at about the same time I was served with 2 separate disciplinary allegations. The 1st read that I 'used my office as a constable to seek evidence for a civil case.' I had a god-daughter of about 8, who had her nostril bitten off by a dog. The surgeon removed an earlobe and tried to make a nostril but it failed. So the poor kid was missing a nostril and an earlobe. My friend, her Dad, understandably wanted something done, as anyone would.

I knew that I could be leaving myself open for criticism and allegations of a conflict of interest if I were to be the officer in the case. So I asked another PC on my section if he would act as the O.I.C and I would help out by taking statements and some investigating. I saw nothing wrong with this arrangement. I was fully aware that I was a lowly PC and I would therefore err on the side of caution.

I eventually traced about a dozen other people (no mean feat) who had also been bitten by the same dog. I was determined to see this dangerous dog destroyed and I took most of the statements. The dog's owner was taken before the court and the dog was ordered to be destroyed. There never was a civil case so that allegation was going nowhere.

The other 2nd allegation read, 'You did, whilst off duty, call your sister in law a cow.' My sister in law was Liz, the ranting and raving one, that I told of at the beginning but she and my brother were now divorcing. What absolute nonsense, eh?

Both discipline complaints were being investigated by the same superintendent. Superintendent B, we'll call him.

Then, at that time, an ex-girlfriend of mine went to the police station to get someone to sign her passport photos. Superintendent A just happened to see her at the front counter of the enquiry office and he fell over himself, to take her into his own office. Do you think you could expect to walk into any police station unannounced for a passport signature and receive the same treatment from a superintendent? I think not! She was a very attractive girl and he had a reputation for a roving eye and flirting with young females. There is more to this but I have decided not to go into any further detail. He quizzes her as to why she's not seeing me anymore and then asks where she's working and she tells him.

The next thing, she starts getting phone calls at work from Superintendent B, who is investigating me, asking/pleading for her to meet him. Reluctantly, she agrees to meet him at lunchtime on the seafront in his private car, to get rid of him. He says he's investigating me, over the rubbish I have stated. She asks how on earth she can help him and he outrageously says, "You went out with him for a long time. Did you ever know him to do anything wrong?" She says, "Tom might be a lot of things but he is no bent copper. If that is what you are looking for?" He says, "Think about it and I can ring you again sometime."

It was nothing more than a malicious fishing expedition, to try and stitch me up! We were not even speaking at the time but she loyally rings me and says, "Can you get this superintendent off my back?" I was fuming but something else happens. Superintendent A calls me into his office and says, "You have to go to HQ and I don't know what for." What, the boss does not know? I'd never been called to HQ in the 13 years I'd been a cop!

I go to HQ and I see Superintendent C. He tells me my name has been chosen at random and I'm suddenly being posted to Hastings, 50 miles away. It was obvious straight away, who was behind all this skulduggery, Superintendent A and he wanted me moved.

So Superintendent C says, "Well it might be good for you. A new start and you do have 2 disciplinary charges on you." I said, "Just hang on a bit. Are you not presuming my guilt before the result of the enquiries?" I then told him about Superintendents A and B and the pestering of my ex-girlfriend and daring to ask her if she knew of anything I'd done wrong. I said, "It is nothing but a witch hunt and victimisation. I'm expected to believe my name randomly came out of a computer for a move to the other end of the county. If I am sent to Hastings, I will take a witness statement from my ex-girlfriend and file a complaint." He said, "What are you on tomorrow?" I said "Day off" and he said, "I shall speak to the deputy chief constable and I will ring you." The next morning he rang and he said that it was all off. I would not be going anywhere.

That same day, both Superintendents A and B were at HQ to see the deputy chief constable. I reckon it was for a slap on the wrist.

STOPPED BY THE POLICE

At this time, my Mam and her husband Pop were on holiday with me from Darlington. A few days after the HQ business, I took them out to the Worthing police social club. It was a nice quiet atmosphere in there and they always enjoyed it, as was the case that night, but not what was to follow.

On the way home, I was driving along the seafront when I was stopped by a police traffic car, with a sergeant and PC, whom I knew. I was asked if I'd been drinking and I said I'd had a couple of beers. I then remembered that the last time I'd been to the police club was on a Sunday lunchtime. I'd left my car in front of the police station and I returned to it but on the way, I saw a friend and I stopped to talk to him. I suddenly saw the same cops come shooting out of the police yard, in the same traffic car.

It was obvious now they'd watched me come out of the club and knew where my car was parked. They gave me a minute or two to get going and shot off after me but they did not account for me being delayed talking to my friend. So afraid their cover was blown, they must have thought, we'll get him next time and the next time was now.

I reckoned Superintendent A had put the newly promoted and undoubtedly obliging sergeant, on special duty together with a PC, just to get me. You see sergeants are not normally crewed with

PC's and I'd seen them together twice now. What is normal police practice is that if you are after a cop, preferably a rank higher is tasked with the job.

I let my frustrations get the better of me and when they requested a sample of breath, I refused. I was arrested and taken away from Mam and Pop to the police station. At the nick, I refused to give a sample of blood or urine. (No breath test machines back then.) Mam and Pop had been taken home. My car was kept at the police station and I was told that I'd be reported for summons for refusing to give a breath test at the scene and refusing to give a sample at the police station. I was released and shown the door.

When I got back home my Mam was understandably upset. She was in her 70s and had just seen her son, a cop arrested for refusing a breath test. She was worried I might lose my job. I reassured her I would not. I was confident that would be the case, going by what happened to others in a similar situation, at that time. (Nowadays, you'd be unwise to be so confident.) Everyone would know it was a fit-up. Cops did not usually get stopped in their own area in the 80s and asked for breath samples. Any cop on a drink driving charge normally had been in an accident and was over the limit. I don't really know if I'd have been over. You can never tell for sure until you see the reading. As I refused everything, I did not get any such reading. I'll tell you this, I would not have driven my elderly Mam and Pop if I didn't think I was safe to do so.

In the morning, it was my day off but HQ rang me and said they wanted to see me again, the following day. I went to HQ and saw the same Superintendent C again. This time he said in view of the pending refusing a breath test charge, I would be posted immediately to Hove but only temporarily and then this time, I was going to be posted to Gatwick Airport. I hated the prospect of Gatwick as it is not a town and I did not want to go there one bit. It was known as a punishment posting.

I said to Superintendent C the following; "It is obvious to everyone that Superintendent A has sent the boys out after me because a few days ago he got his wrist slapped together with Superintendent B for being so stupid. He wasn't going to take that. Two days later, I get stopped by a newly promoted sergeant and asked for a breath sample, when I haven't been in an accident. Everyone will know, including you that I've been fitted up. Now I am not in as good a bartering position as I was two days ago when we did a deal but I still have something to barter with. I do not want to go to Gatwick. If you send me to Hastings, (I had never been to Hastings but it had to be better than Gatwick, I thought) as you were going to and drop the refusing to give a breath test at the scene, I will shut my mouth about Superintendent A and B. I'll also plead guilty to refusing to give the sample at the police station."

Superintendent C said that he would again speak to the deputy chief constable and ring me the next day. He did call and he said, "Ok, you've got a deal." Is it every day that a deputy chief constable does a deal, (twice in a few days) with an alleged wayward PC if there is nothing that might cause embarrassment and shame to the force? I think not!

I choose not to name the superintendents involved but only because it is unnecessary and in consideration of the passage of time, it is now of no importance to me whatsoever. I also know that at least one of the superintendents is dead and I wish to respect only his family. I do this in the full knowledge that libel law in the UK does not apply to a deceased person. Therefore, I believe my decision is a gracious one.

Later, both discipline complaints were found to be totally unsubstantiated and of course, there was no further action taken.

I will never know if my ex-sister-in-law first made contact with the police, to make her vindictive complaint or if she was contacted by Superintendent B, as my ex-girlfriend was and encouraged. Needless to say, I have never heard of any other cop being served with a complaint, that he called a member of his family a name when he was off duty. No wonder a deal was struck with me, TWICE. Shameful!

POSTED TEMPORARILY TO HOVE

Within a few days, I was settled in temporarily at Hove. The bosses were nice to me as were everyone else. I was travelling in my car still because it would be a couple of months before my case was before the court. I had to move swiftly now or I could find myself disqualified from driving and not being able to get to Hove without difficulty, for a 6 am start.

I had to put my house up for sale and find one at Hastings. There was some good news though, the police would be paying for everything, removal, estate agent, solicitor, curtains and new carpets.

I have withheld something up to now that was going to change my private life. I had been single for about 6 years but now I was going to be settling down with a new partner. Do you recall the twins at Darlington, who called upon me when the train had been damaged and the driver had been injured and who got the £50 reward? Well, the little girl, Jackie, was now 23 and I had been dating her for about 18 months. She had been married but now was divorced and she had a 4-year-old daughter, Johanna. She and her family had lived next door to my Mam but her Mam had re-married and moved. The council house had been transferred to Jackie. I had gotten to know her on my visits to Mam. She was moving in with me, with her daughter within a week or two.

So I pulled out all the stops and I very quickly found a new detached house in Hastings, within 5 minutes walking distance of the police station. A PC friend of mine at Worthing bought my house, which had been on the books of 2 estate agents but I had found a buyer myself. One of the agents who knew the police would have paid found the temptation too much and said that if I agreed to say they'd sold it, he'd give me half the fee. Had he not stopped to think, that he was proposing to a serving cop, to defraud the Sussex Police? I asked if he'd give it to me before or after we shared a cell in Lewes HMP? The other, I also told him to get lost, when he asked if I'd allow him to put his sold sign up. Are these guys in a different world where fraud has ceased to exist? My ex-girlfriend was right. I was never a bent cop!

At the end of November 1983, I thanked the bosses at Hove Police Station for their understanding. My report from them said that I had worked well the short time I'd been with them.

We loaded the removal van and Jackie, Johanna and I were off along the coast to Hastings. Let the battle begin!

CHAPTER 9

POSTED TO HASTINGS

Once settled in my new home, I took stock of the situation. I'd previously been living in a terraced 3 bedroom house and now I had a bigger, new detached home. Property is cheaper in East Sussex. At that time, a rent allowance was payable from the police and it was assessed on the council rates for that property. Now, I'd be receiving a lot more rent allowance than I had been and enough to cover my increased mortgage. The home was fully carpeted and had been paid for by the police. My initial chat with the Hastings cops revealed that there was loads of overtime to be had, the opposite of Worthing. I was only 5 minutes walk from the nick and so I was prepared for the time when I lost my licence and it would have little effect. It had not turned out so bad after all. I'd be better off financially in Hastings than at Worthing and that proved to be the case. Unexpectedly, it had turned out to be better than a promotion.

What I thought was, I won't wait to be set up again. I'll drink a bottle of whisky and wrap the car around a lamp-post and wait for the police to arrive. Then I'll be posted to the opposite end of the county 70 miles away to Chichester and make some more money. Then I thought, no they wouldn't stand for it a second time. Just wait and see how this goes first and make future plans later!

As normal, I still retained my all-important sense of humour, telling my new workmates, that I believed I had battled the enemy here before. Everyone knows, the Battle of Hastings was in 1066 but when in 1066? It was on 14 October, my birthday. Not 1066 though, 1949! My middle name is William, who fought Harold. My right eye sometimes gets sore. Harold was killed with an arrow to his eye. I thought I better be extra-cautious now that I was back in Hastings after 900 years and I quickly changed my aftershave to Aramis!

On 4th December 1983, I presented myself at Hastings police stationed and joined my new section on a late shift at 10 pm. I had been initially told that my first day would be 9 am to 5 pm but I said I saw no need for that. I was not a new cop who needed to be shown around and eased into the job. I was just new to Hastings and that was no problem either. I figured that if I had a radio and a street map, I could walk out the nick and maybe be back very soon, being directed by my first prisoner.

I knew immediately when I set foot in Hastings that I was going to be happy as a cop there and when my astute copper's nose sniffed the air, I could smell criminals. This was to prove to be so because compared to my last 13 years in Worthing, I was going to enjoy a faster pace which I thrived on and in a mini Brighton. My only concern was the Hastings hills. I might struggle sometimes with my asthma, especially when I lost my licence and foot patrol would be the only option but I was to discover any concern was unfounded.

I liked all the guys on the section straight away, including the inspector and 3 sergeants. They welcomed me with open arms and nobody seemed to give a jot what had brought me to Hastings, just that I was there and as I was a seasoned cop, I did not need to be guided. There were several PC's with service under their belts and they were long term established enough, to be playfully mischievous characters too. I was to go on to share many laughs with those fine men. I thought I'm going to slot in here without any trouble and that was to be the case.

The following week, I was on a late shift and now I was introduced to the 9 am to 5 pm team, including Superintendent Ray Barr. This superintendent, divisional commander, was a true gentleman at all times and treated everyone respectfully, not quite what I had been used to at Worthing. I was surprised at how warm and welcoming he was. He certainly didn't seem concerned about why I'd come to Hastings or he might not have said, " We have a nice comfortable bar and social club here which all the members enjoy." He then said something which I particularly noted, he said,

"Do you mind if I ask, have you been to court yet?" I told him, "No." He said," It's come down the line to look after you and so if you lose your driving licence, we'll try and put you in a car with someone who can drive. You're too useful to be on foot?" Blimey, I thought, talk about being fair." My respect for him remains and he will always be, Mr Barr to me. He was a man of his word and sure enough, I was almost always in a car.

COURT AND THE POLICE DISCIPLINE HEARING

In about March, my case came up at Steyning Magistrates Court. I kept my word and said nothing except, "Guilty." I came away with a reasonable £100 fine and a 1-year driving disqualification. I also had to appear before the chief constable on the disciplinary charge of discreditable conduct, for the refusal of the breath sample at the police station. This is always the case if there is court action of that nature involving a cop. I pleaded guilty and I was given a 'reprimand' and that was the end of the matter.

During the hearing with the chief constable, he was extremely nice to me and not the same to Superintendent A in my presence, who had to be there as my divisional commander. At one point he rebuked him and dismissed him from the hearing. Afterwards, the chief constable had an informal friendly chat with me saying, "Put it behind you and good luck in Hastings." He obviously knew more than he was letting on about. I have nothing but the utmost respect for that chief constable.

214

I did put it behind me and as you will read, it did not affect my police performance or private life.

A CHANGE OF FORTUNE

Jackie was taking driving lessons and passed her test the first time. I had gotten rid of my car. Then an unexpected and somewhat odd bit of luck came our way. Jackie had been taking an interest in cars and in particular, the new shape Ford Escort, which had just been released and she mentioned it but I said that we only had £1,500.

About this time, a Vernon's football pools collection guy called on us and asked if we were interested. I said that I wasn't but Jackie said," I used to watch my Dad do them. I'd like to." So we did and we decided we'd do 4 lines and adopted a type of system. I would fill two lines in, both being of numbers that meant something to us, like birthdates etc. She was to do the other 2 lines but none of our X's had to be on the same line. Within a couple of weeks, we had the 8 out of 11 and our payout was just a few pounds short of £3,500. With the £1,500 we had in the bank we had £5,000, the exact price of the car Jackie wanted. An interesting point was that Jackie made an error in her winning line. Of the 8 winning X's she had done, one of them was on the same line as mine. That was not what we agreed but if she had not made the error, she would only have had 7 out of the 11. Jackie said that if we had done Littlewoods instead of Vernon's, we'd have won £24,000. However, we might have fallen short because they were 8 out of 10. I reminded her that had it been Zetters, we would have won

£800. We were both chuffed to bits and who wouldn't be? The same day we got the cheque we were in the car showroom and Jackie was saying, "I'll have that one in blue." I still find it remarkable.

The salesman must have thought it was all a bit strange. Jackie being a new driver was nervous about driving it because it was a different car from the one she had learnt on. She understandably said that she did not want to have a test drive in front of us and would like to drive it as and when she was psyched up for it. Of course, I could not drive it. We asked for it to be delivered and he left it on the drive without ever having seen either of us drive it. Furthermore, we said we could not drop him back! Jackie proved to be a very good driver and I now had a chauffeur at my disposal at home, as well as at work. I was really starting to like Hastings now.

It got even better when a month or two later, I won £1,000, which was the 1st prize in the Sussex Police, one-off lottery. So that was £4,500 we had won, the equivalent of £10,600 now.

A big presentation with drinks was held at HQ Lewes and the chief constable presented me with the cheque and the runners up were there too. There were loads of bosses there and I was the only one who dared say a few words, as normal. The promoter was Chief Superintendent Alan Skinner. On the day my winning ticket was drawn, he rang Hastings from HQ and left a message for me to ring him but he did not say what it was about. I was in the canteen when I got the message to ring him and I did it straight away. What I said in part of my speech, was that the switchboard operator gave me the message and I said to her, "What does the chief superintendent want?" and she said, "I don't know would you like to ring him?" I said, that I had said to her, "I wouldn't want to ring him for a thousand pounds." I continued saying, "but I did ring him and..... well, thanks for the thousand pounds."

OPERATION VULCAN AND I BECOME A GAOLER

Around about this time, it was announced that because of the HMP overcrowding, remanded in custody prisoners would be temporarily housed in police custody, an unprecedented scheme. Superintendent Barr asked to see me again but I had no idea what he was about to say. He said he would like me to become a full-time gaoler and be part of 'Operation Vulcan,' as it would come to be known. He said, "I cannot use probationers with these guys. I need experienced officers."

My first reaction was, as I had been on many escorts to various prisons with Matt Wilson and I had an insight into what it might be like, to be cooped up with these men, I would rather not be part of it. I already believed there was a difference between them and us but I would soon come to realise the gap was much wider than I thought. I had joined the police to be a cop and not to be locked up with those I nicked. I much preferred to be in their company as short a time as possible and get back on the streets to gather up some more. Superintendent Barr had shown me such kindness and I owed him. I said, "Of course I'll do it, sir." He said, "Good."

Very soon after seeing the superintendent, I started my new role as a full-time gaoler in the Hastings police station cellblock. I would be working the same shift pattern alongside another PC.

To enter the cellblock, first, you must pass through a heavy metal bar gate. Once inside there is a reception desk and to the left of that is another metal gate giving access to 6 male cells, half with a toilet and half without. Also in this area is a room normally used as an interview room but during Vulcan, it would be used as a TV room and for socialising. An open shower was in an alcove in the corridor. To the right of the reception desk is a room used for doctor examination's and photographing prisoners.

There is another gate that accesses two more female cells with toilets and a gaoler's office. These two cells would be now used to house any male prisoner arrested in Hastings, normally only there for a few hours or maybe overnight, as in the case of a drunk. We Vulcan gaolers would not have anything to do with Hastings prisoners, there were regular gaolers for that. Further down the corridor was an exercise yard. Throughout Vulcan, no female prisoners would be held at Hastings, they would be taken to Bexhill.

All prisoners to come to us would be known as Operation Vulcan inmates. (Vulcan's) They would be from London and only remand prisoners, meaning those who have been charged and have been remanded into custody by a court to await trial. No convicted prisoner ever came our way. The offences they were in custody for pending trial could be anything from petty crime such as shoplifting, criminal damage, and minor drugs offences, to the
218

more serious offences of armed robbery and murder etc. I would come into direct contact with all of these. I found those charged with petty stuff, seemed to be the ones who gave us more trouble and problems than any major crime offender ever did. I can only think the reason for this was that those charged with a serious crime, accepted the inevitability of their fate and complied, whilst the petty offender retained his arrogance knowing he would be free again relatively soon.

These prisoners would normally be collected weekly and be taken to their home court to be remanded again and then be returned to us. Some would leave to be sentenced or be sent to other holding facilities and so our turnover was frequent. We would have 12 Vulcan prisoners, two to a cell and those without a toilet, would have to push a buzzer to be allowed out to use a facility. This would be at night as most of the time through the day, they would be out of the cell. With the gate locked they would be free to mix in the open cells, corridor, TV room and exercise yard. So when my colleague or I entered via the gate, we were then alone in the area as they roamed freely around us. It was prudent for us not to carry our truncheons but there were the buzzers we could hit if needed, I never did but I came close to it a few times.

The prisoners would enter the block handcuffed to one another and escorted by prison officers. We would search, document and book them in upon their arrival. Any property they could retain, cigarettes, sweets etc. would be handed over to them and the rest was bagged up and stored. They wore their own clothes as remand prisoners always do but no ties, belts, shoelaces etc. They were allowed frequent visits, which one of us would supervise and it would be within eyeshot but not earshot. All such visits were to take place in a visitor's room, which had been the juvenile detention room and was situated near to the reception desk.

Meals were provided by the police canteen staff and would be taken in their cells or the TV/social room, left to their choice. All the cutlery was plastic, as were their plates and mugs. At tea times we would put a big metal teapot on a trolley with mugs, sugar and milk in a plastic jug, wheel it into them and they would help themselves. I nearly freaked out once, when a colleague had prepared the teas. On my entering the wing after him, my eyes zoomed on to a glass milk bottle sitting on the tea trolley. There was everyday stuff too that was seemingly innocent enough, under normal circumstances but for their safety was withheld, metal coat hangers could be bent to strangle for example. They were only allowed the single sheet tracing paper type, toilet paper. The soft rolls can be twisted into long lengths and then plaited as in a rope, with enough strength by far to hang a person. All these things we Vulcan gaolers had to quickly and on the hoof work out, pick up from full-time gaolers or carry forward from our own past occasional gaoler experiences. There were no prior courses or lectures to attend or indeed any time to arrange such. No cop had ever done this type of gaoler work in the past, the only ones who could have really prepared us, were prison officers but that did not happen.

For many months I was off the streets, doing a job I would never have chosen and I spent long periods with those, I would rather not have been with. Although, I was spat at and on one occasion quite seriously injured, I was never afraid, even when alone with 12. The spitter was shipped out immediately and re-housed within the HMP system, as was my attacker but not before I charged him with assault occasioning actual bodily harm, a more serious charge than an assault on police. He got time added on to the sentence which he was given for his original offence. His attack was completely unprovoked. I had no trouble from him whatsoever and he had been with us for a couple of weeks. I was laying out the lunches when behind me I heard shouting and I turned around. He head-butted me so violently I almost collapsed. My face was swollen and black and blue. He later said that he'd been refused a visit by another officer and had been so mad, he decided he would take it out on the first cop he saw and that was the unsuspecting me. That is the mentality of some of these people.

On the whole, the Vulcan prisoners seemed to prefer to be in police custody to that of HMP. For a start, they were mostly out of their cells all day and with no overcrowding. The food and the flexible visiting times were better too.

Throughout my time engaged on the Vulcan duties, I witnessed many things that convinced me of my, us and them, theory. Some either sickened or repulsed. What I did know was, I was pleased that I had not chosen to be a prison officer. I could see an end in sight, whereas they faced 30 years. I felt they were also serving time. I grew to value and pity our HMP staff in equal measures.

I will now outline some of the daily occurrences I was to experience. For some, it may destroy any idea that these characters, can be in any way compared to likeable rogue Norman Stanley Fletcher, portrayed in the TV comedy Porridge, as played by the extremely talented funnyman, the late Ronnie Barker.

On one occasion, I heard an argument in full swing coming from the TV room. I hurried to find they were arguing as to what channel they would view. Things were getting heated and so I unplugged the portable TV and picked it up, to remove it to the gaoler's office. I then said that they should all go to their cells until everyone had calmed down. They all had been pre-warned on their initial arrival, that this action would be taken to ensure the maintenance of good order. They reluctantly complied and I thought, I'll give it an hour and I'll reinstall the TV and open up the cells again. Problem resolved, hopefully.

It seemed that I was a lot more forgiving than one of my inmates. I was in the office when a cell buzzer sounded. I went to the cell, dropped the hatch and the inmate said, "Can I speak to you boss?" We had never told them to address us in any certain way. They seemed to choose boss because it was acceptable and does not sound too submissive, I suppose. As far as I was concerned, I did not care what they called me, as long as it was not offensive. I said, "Yes, what is it?" He said, "In the office?" I opened the cell and took him into the office. He said, " If you take the volume switch off his radio, he's got cannabis stuffed into it." He was referring to the inmate he had been arguing with. He said, "I only want you to leave it a bit, so he doesn't know I grassed him up." I agreed but despised him and he was returned to the cell.

I discussed it with my mate and we decided how we would deal with this. It must have been a relatively tiny amount of cannabis to be concealed in a small transistor radio volume switch. We would rather he kept it, in preference to having a disruption or a riot on our hands. We thought the cannabis was probably smoked in the open part of the exercise yard. I didn't much care if he had a bit of cannabis for his personal use, although I was not about to condone it, whilst in police custody. I decided I'd give the informant a bit longer to think about it and see if he spoke to me again. I also hoped if we did not act straight away, if we did check, the cannabis might have gone. After an hour or so I opened up the cells and put the TV back.

The next day I noticed the two who had argued appeared to be at least exchanging words. I was half expecting the informant to ask to speak to me again and ask if I could now overlook it but he did not. I was not going to risk taking him into the office again, for fear of arousing the inmate's suspicion. So later that shift, it was arranged for a cell search team of PCs, not engaged in gaoler's duties, to come in and do a 'routine' cell search. That was done and the tiny bit of cannabis was discovered.

Nobody connected the informant. The owner of the cannabis had it confiscated and was given a police caution for the possession and that was it. He did not deserve another charge being put on him. As for the grass who grassed about the grass, well I liked the guy who owned the cannabis better than him. You may have heard the saying, 'honour amongst thieves' which makes them sound like Robin Hood figures. Don't believe it!

MUM'S THE WORD

I recall one occasion when a new set of Vulcan's arrived. I had a quick look at their files as they were being brought in. I saw one guy was in for armed robbery. I looked at his mugshot and what a mug! He looked tough and mean with a flat boxer's nose. I thought, Mmm! I might have to keep an eye on him. I started booking them in and I came to him. He was bigger than I first thought and reminded me of Arthur Mullard. (Actor) He moved forward and I told him to put any property he had on the counter.

What he said, took me totally by surprise. He said, "Haven't you got lovely eyes?" I sputtered and then burst out laughing. So did he, the other inmates, cops and prison officers who were all waiting patiently. It was hilarious. He was 100% gay and as docile as could be and I never had any bother from him. He helped in the running of the wing by doing all the sweeping, serving teas and generally being helpful. All the others called him Mum and he seemed to warm to it i.e. Q. "Is there any more tea in the pot, Mum?" Reply, "For you love, I'll squeeze it and anything else if you ask nicely?"... Laughter! As for the armed robbery, it was a domestic dispute with someone he knew and he threatened him with a knife and took some money. It might have even been an ex-lover. I never found out what he got but it could not have been a lot.

He really did think he was a beautiful and dainty female though. I can give one good example of why I came to that conclusion. They were all in the TV room and one guy was reading the Sun newspaper. Well, more like just looking at the pictures because he was looking at a Page 3 topless model. He said, "Mum, look at me." Mum stopped and looked at the guy and he looked at Mum and then at the paper and back again at Mum. He then said, "Mum, I swear there's a bird here and she is your double. You could be twins," trying to wind him up. Mum said, "Give me a look then? He looked at the young pretty busty model and after quite a long while, he said, "Oh! F... off my hair's not that long!" If anyone else compared them on a 'spot the difference,' I can guarantee you, that the last one spotted would be the length of the hair. He truly believed there was a similarity.

In the beginning, he was in a cell that did not have a toilet. Every single night at lights out, about 10 minutes later, his buzzer would go for him to be let out for the toilet. He would come out with a towel folded around his waist, like a micro mini skirt. He would shimmy, very slowly up the corridor. He would stop occasionally and make out he was looking at something or he'd adjust the towel, whilst looking at me to see if I was watching him. I would see him out the corner of my eye, as I was leaned on the cell door, looking straight ahead. Before lights out, I'd say, "Are you going to the toilet because I'm busy in the office?" He'd say, "I can't go if I don't want to go." 10 minutes later, his buzzer would go again. I wasn't going to have this every night. So as soon as a cell with a toilet became vacant, I had it earmarked for him and his cellmate.

One evening after lights out, I went to check on them all. You could look through the spy hole and see clearly into the cell. When I got to his cell, I looked in and saw he was bent over the bed and he and his cellmate were involved in a sexual act. It didn't shock me because of my previous visual encounters, whilst detecting gross indecency in male public toilets. In fact, the inmates were not committing any offence, they were consenting and it was in private. Such matters had ceased to shock me but of course, to say the least, they were not to my taste. I know the majority of officers without my experience would have been indeed shocked. I knew it went on and I would not be mentioning it now perhaps but for what happened next.

A few days later, I had to sit in on a visit of a young attractive female and it was with the guy, who I had seen with Mum. The girl was his girlfriend and during the visit, although the majority of the time out of earshot, I knew they were making plans for their wedding day. This was confirmed, when I heard him telling the others how much he loved her and that they were to be married when he got out.

None of the others knew what he and Mum got up to after lights out and he clearly gave the impression of being totally heterosexual. He could well have been bisexual, when free. If he were totally heterosexual on the outside, then he was in the same category as the great majority of the men I caught in toilets. In other words, he would have preferred his partner to be a female but if that was not readily available, he settled for the next best thing, exactly in the same way as the majority I caught.

After what I had seen, I was repulsed by his affectionate show of love to his girlfriend as I supervised their visit. I could not help thinking, poor girl if only she knew! That's enough on that subject.
226

SHHH! KEEP NICE AND QUIET

One inmate who came into our charge was a London black guy. He was well built and must have been at least 6'4". I'm 5'10" and I felt like a little kid when I was next to him. He was charged with murder and had strangled another male. He lived in a block of flats and he went to a neighbour and asked him to turn down the music he was playing. It continued, he returned and so he told me, the guy 'disrespected him.' So he strangled and murdered him. He then went to the local police station and gave himself up. I thought I'm going to try and be extra respectful to this guy! Honestly, I never feared him and he never once gave me cause to. I treated him exactly the same as the others.

I recall he had a florescent blue suit amongst his possessions and he asked me for a coat hanger. I told him that he was not allowed one and why. He said, "I want to take care of my suit because I want it for when I get out." It flashed through my mind that it might not be in fashion when he got out and he might like to be dressed like all of us, in a spacesuit. I thought it best to say, "We'll fold it up and wrap it up nicely and it'll only need to be hung up for an hour or two and it'll be fine." Gladly, he settled for that.

I met many murderers and they all struck me as looking so normal. There are exceptions of course but I'm talking majority. The only difference between them and I, is in a moment of madness and often in a split second, they lost control and committed the most heinous of all crimes. They do not all have wide staring eyes as in the mugshots you see. That photo was taken in harsh light conditions, not smiling and after all, what did they have to smile about right then. Most likely it was taken with a flash camera. We all might look scary if we were subjected to the same treatment.

One night a drunk was arrested in town and he was put in one of the two cells on the opposite side of the block, the two that were reserved for that purpose. As a lot of them do, he was making a hell of a racket banging the door, screaming and shouting. It was little wonder he had awoken and was preventing all the Vulcan prisoners from sleeping. A buzzer from a cell was activated and it was the big black guy, charged with the strangulation. He said, "Who's making all the noise?" I said, "It's a drunk who's been nicked. I've tried everything to try and get him to pipe down but nothing is going to make him keep quiet." He said, "Put him in here with me and I'll make him nice and quiet for you!" I'd got to know him a lot better by then and I could not resist saying, "You're in enough trouble already?" He replied, "Then it don't matter, then, do it?" and chuckled.

A NEST OF VIPERS

Amongst one group of inmates, we had were 4 men who were jointly charged with the same offence, that of importing Krugerrands and avoiding the VAT. My opinion was that this gang should never have been allowed to be housed together but I was a PC and so what could I do. All in their late 40s, they were a cocky, slippery little mob and I decided to distance myself and play everything by the book with them, no deviation whatsoever. I sussed them out, that given an inch they would take a mile. They tried everything to ingratiate themselves with me and other gaolers, with whom I shared my concerns. They were continually in huddles as soon as we unlocked them. They had bundles of court papers and would whisper for long periods, obviously to concoct a plan for their up and coming court appearance or more like performance. I overheard them on many occasions referring to customs officers in derogatory terms. It was customs and excise who had nicked and charged them, not the police. They seemed to think that the customs officers were amateurs, which contradicted my impression of them. I believed that they should be feared because they appeared to have far more manpower and resources to chuck at a case than the police ever did.

It quickly became apparent that the leader, of this nest of vipers, was a guy called Roy Garner. As I recall he could only have been about 5'7", medium build and balding. The others would fuss around him, such as, "Do you want another tea, Roy? I'll get that for you, Roy. Here have this chair, Roy." As they were remand prisoners, they had money in their property, hundreds of pounds, and could buy stuff from outside. The driver/orderly, like Matt at Worthing, would be given a shopping list for all 12 and would have to shop for them. The main items were stuff like cigarettes, sweets and soft drinks but it could include loads of other items, such as pens and writing paper. The 4s lists were longer than all the others put together and especially Garner's. He used to buy enough for everyone and he would dish out, cigarettes and sweets to all the Vulcan's, every time a shop was done. It was all to impress and to curry favour. What a Flash Harry he was!

GHANIAN DRUG SMUGGLER

A black guy from Ghana was with us, at the same time as the Garner mob and he'd been yet another, nicked by customs at Gatwick for importing drugs He was a guy who was on the very bottom rung of life. A drugs baron would get these poor guys and give them a stash of drugs, get them a passport and pay them a ridiculously small amount of money but a fortune to him and the offer of more when he returned. He would fly to Gatwick and when he got there, the customs would have a team of officers waiting for the Ghana flight because they knew for sure what these guys were arriving in the UK for. It was like collecting sweets from a candy store. They nicked them in droves. These guys were known as 'mules'. The drug baron's very rarely got caught. Their theory is to send many over and if only one escapes the net, they are into profit.

This guy hardly spoke any English and was understandably bemused and he was forever crying. His family would not know what became of him and he'd been in custody for weeks. Garner said, "I'll pay for a phone call to Ghana for him, whatever it costs." A phone number was obtained and it was for a shop and the black guy said that if we rang that number they would send a runner to get his wife. It could take maybe an hour to get his wife to the phone. Garner said, "Keep the line open or ring them back, whatever you want to do." To save my time, I chose to ring twice. I took the money out of Garner's property. I cannot remember how much it was but I do recall that it was not cheap.

My opinion at the time was that Garner did not do it out of compassion. It was done to impress and he may have had a business interest in drug smuggling, as well as Krugerrands!

LITTLE MR BIG TESTS THE WATER

One of the other 4 said to me, "Roy's a multi-millionaire. You want to see the house he lives in and he's got others too. He's got a beautiful yacht and a Rolls Royce and god knows what else." I did not comment. Then Garner starts trying his hand with me and I remember in particular this, "My club is next door to ? police station. (I cannot remember which one but it was in London) All the boys from next door come to my club. When we get out we're going to have a big celebration. Why don't you and your mate come up and join us? It won't cost you a penny it'll be all on me." Another time he said to me, "Thanks for what you do for us. What do you drink? I'll get a crate of whatever you drink sent to your house, whisky, brandy or whatever you fancy." I said, "Thanks but I don't drink." I think he got the message because he didn't try it on again. They were with us for weeks and I was sick to death of them.

DOUBLE TROUBLE

I was always vigilant when supervising an inmate's visit. In Garner's case, I recall something that caused me enough concern to make me decide that I would watch him like a hawk when supervising a visit from one particular person. I was going to try not to blink when these two were around each other. That person was his brother, his identical twin brother and I mean identical.

231

The first time I saw his brother I did a double-take. I could hardly believe it because they were like two peas in a pod. I knew by then that Garner was cunning enough, to use any tool in his kit to give him an advantage.

I thought how easy it would be to fix an alibi if one had a body double and Garner was wily enough to have twigged that long ago. There never was a switch attempted, whilst he with us but I thought nothing should be taken for granted when it came to the unlikeable Garner and his three cohorts. Throughout Vulcan, there was never anyone, I disliked being around more, than him and his three co-conspirators and that included those charged with murder.

The cocky 4 got their just deserts and were all found guilty. I believe Garner got 4 years but there was another aspect to this part of the story. Whilst Garner was serving his time, he had more time added to his sentence for bribing a prison officer. The officer was also convicted of accepting the bribe and he too was sentenced to imprisonment.

You have to wonder, did it start with, "Thanks for what you do for us. What do you drink? I'll get a crate of whatever you drink sent to your house, whisky, brandy or whatever you fancy."

GARNER FINALLY GETS HIS COMEUPPANCE

About 5 years later, I read this;

'Man Sentenced in Britain's Biggest Cocaine Case March 24, 1989.

LONDON (AP) _ A judge sentenced a man to 22 years in prison on Thursday, for conspiring to smuggle more than $172 million in cocaine into Britain.

Two Americans, Brian Van Den Breen and Robert Cermac, also were jailed for 12 and seven years respectively for their part in importing 880 pounds of the drug in 1986 - the largest amount ever smuggled into Britain.

In passing sentence, on businessman Roy Garner and the Americans, Judge Kenneth Machin said substantial sentences were needed to "make it clear beyond peradventure that drug-trafficking will be stamped out by the courts. " He said, "The drugs trade causes untold misery, damage and sometimes death to the takers of drugs."

Addressing Garner, the judge said, "I am quite satisfied that but for your involvement in this conspiracy, a huge quantity of cocaine would never have come to the United Kingdom."

A jury found the three guilty on Wednesday, following a trial at the Old Bailey Criminal Court.

The court heard that Garner, 52, ran part of the operation from prison after he was jailed in connection with a gold fraud case.

Van Den Breen, 40, of London, and Cermak, 28, of Key Largo, Fla., pleaded guilty to taking part in the conspiracy. A 43-year-old woman, who could not be identified under court rules, also was found guilty of conspiracy to supply cocaine. She will be sentenced at a later date.

The drugs were shipped from Colombia to the Cornish coast, off England in 1986 and then taken to London for distribution but when customs officials confiscated the cocaine about a year later, only 120 pounds was left.'

A RARE COLLECTORS ITEM

I must tell this funny little story involving the driver/orderly, who was in his mid-30s. The job was not fantastic money and to subsidise his wages, he would clean cops private cars when it was quiet for a couple of quid, mine being one of them. He had been doing it for some time when he said for whatever reason that he wasn't going to do them anymore. We were all peeved and moaned at him but he stuck to his guns and said, "No." A couple of weeks went by and I saw him at the car wash bay. He was washing a DS's private car. I stopped and said, "What's this then, selected clientele?" He replied, "That's where you're wrong then Mr clever clogs. If you really want to know it's a Toyota Celica."

I RETURN TO NORMAL POLICE DUTIES

On the 10th April 1984, I was sent to a ladies toilet on the seafront and took details of a handbag theft, including the details of credit cards etc. A female had gone into a cubicle to use the toilet and

234

she had placed her handbag on the floor in front of her. A hand came underneath the door and snatched it and disappeared. So you ladies beware and do not put your handbag on the floor.

Other identical thefts had recently taken place and I had the hunch he/she would strike again and soon. So when I returned to the nick, I saw my inspector and told him that I was off the next day but I reckoned there was a good chance of catching the offender. I would be willing to work my day off but for the normal overtime rate. The inspector agreed but later, said that he'd changed his mind because one of my 3 sergeants had been to see him. The sergeant said that I had 'conned' him and I was only trying to get the overtime paid. I was as mad as hell but could do nothing about it OR could I?

The next day at around noon, I said to Jackie, my wife, (who I'd married and officially adopted Johanna) "Do you fancy a walk?" She said, "Where to?" I said, "The seafront." You do know where this is heading now, don't you? We happened to end up at, yes you've got it, the ladies toilets where the handbag had been snatched the previous day. I said, "Let's hang about here for a while." So we, just an ordinary couple, sat on a wall enjoying the sea air in the sunshine.

About 15 minutes went by and I saw a young guy in his mid-20s stroll past the entrance to the toilet. He bent down, tied his shoelace and walked away. I thought he's going, so I better make my mind up and be quick about it too. That was all he did, nothing too suspicious but I didn't like the look of him. Remember my first nick and commendation, the burglar at Worthing 15 years earlier?

That was very similar to this, including I'm off duty of course. So I stop him, introduce myself and ask him who he is and he told me a name. (Later found to be false.) I asked him if he had any ID on him. He said, "No." I said, "No wallet?" He said, "No." I said, "Let's have a look in your pockets then?" and I felt his jacket pockets. He brushed my hand away. I'm committed now and I say harshly and moving close to him, "Don't mess me about!" I felt his pockets again and I took out a wallet and pulled the credit cards out and bingo! They were the cards from the handbag the day before. You're nicked!

I took him to the nick and whilst there I found out something I didn't know. Someone must have thought my hunch had some merit but not worth paying me the overtime because a PC and a WPC had been told to change into plain clothes and were sent to keep observations on the toilets. Unfortunately for them and dead jammy for me, when I got to the toilets they had just left for their lunch. That was their mistake. They should not have left at the relevant time, lunchtime.

The suspect later admitted the offence and 2 others. In court, he was sentenced to 12 months of youth custody. At the conclusion of the case, the chairman of the bench said and I quote; 'I and my colleagues would like to commend the actions of PC Curry, who was off duty at the time and, no doubt, at considerable inconvenience to himself carried out the arrest of the defendant'......'inconvenience?' I wasn't in the convenience, I was outside!

Later Superintendent Barr congratulated me and said that it showed my dedication to duty. I told him I was dedicated but on this occasion, it was not my only motivation. I told him my prime reason was to prove the scurrilous sergeant wrong.

Superintendent Barr said, "Claim the day's overtime."

THE MINERS STRIKE

After my stint as a gaoler, I was relieved to be going back to the job I loved but it would not be long before I was off on another. This one too would be a one I would have preferred not to have had. In the end, I decided that I took an oath to uphold the law and as my father had done by joining up during WW2, I also wanted to do my bit. However, this period would test my loyalties as they had never been tested before, for this was The Miner's Strike!

During 1984, I went to The Miner's Strike in Yorkshire several times. We'd leave Hastings in a coach on Sunday and be billeted at an ex-army camp for the week. On Friday afternoon we'd return home until Sunday again. I, coincidently, attended one pit that my Uncle Tom had worked at but thankfully he'd long since retired. We were out in our vans, about 12 to a van, for 16 hours some days. There was an awful lot of hanging about and dozing off, mainly out of boredom. It was wintertime and freezing when we were out of the van. We sat inside sometimes for hours on end and we would have been freezing in there too, except the driver had to keep the engine running to keep the heater working. I reckon the mileage would have shown 5 miles to the gallon if you'd reckoned it up.

I was lucky in that I never was involved in any major trouble. There was a bit of pushing and shoving but no more. If you watched the TV newscasts, you'd think there was hell on 24/7 but it was edited and they wouldn't get any interest if they just showed us standing about. Where's the news in that? What the viewing public was seeing was the pit buses going in and out, the pickets surging forward, shouting and banging on the side of the bus. Most of that was done for the cameras for effect and to deter/unnerve the strike-breakers (known as scabs) inside the bus.

The buses were not going in and out all day. You might only get one every 8 hours at some pits and with few strike breakers onboard. At some pits I was at, the pickets were as good as gold. Before the pit bus arrived they might say, "Does tha fancy a push the smornin lads?" The reply might be either, "If you like but don't go over the top because we're feeling a bit delicate" or "Yes if you want to try your luck?" The pickets and cops stood around, the buses came and the cameras would roll. The pickets would surge forward and push against us shouting and banging on the bus if they could. The bus would go in, the pushing would stop and so would the cameras. Then there would be maybe more banter i.e. "Ee up, we had thee there, lads" etc. On the other hand, there were pits where there was serious trouble and injuries on both sides.

I recall on one occasion, during the early hours of the morning, when I thought we were in for it for sure. We were at this pit and there were only about 40 of us. The flying pickets started to arrive until there were eventually about 2 to 300 of them, I reckon. The mood on this occasion was seriously hostile and getting worse as the time for the buses approached. Missiles started being thrown in our direction. We 40, had our crash helmets on with visors down and shields at the ready. At night when the lights from the pit buses were first spotted coming towards us in the distance, a shout of, "Here they are, here they are," always went up from the pickets. The shouting began and we could see the lights.

As we small band of 40 stood our ground with shields at the ready, I remembered the film Zulu and I wondered if we would be so lucky. The lights in the distance kept coming and coming and coming. Wait a minute there's too many of them to be the buses. What are they then? Bloody hell, they're all police vans about 20 of them and each would contain 12 coppers. It was like seeing the cavalry coming over the hill! They drove right up to us and like clockwork, the doors opened and within seconds we were 280'ish cops with shields. Phew! Our boss had sent for reinforcements and their timing was perfect. The pickets dispersed and there was little trouble.

At many pits, the relationship was reasonably cordial between cops and pickets but at others, I was told it was not good. There were many occasions when there was unnecessary offensive heckling. Wives of the pickets could be the worst offenders. We were of course, quite rightly, told not to react by responding. I only once heard a retort. A female was yapping on about, "Who's shagging your wives while you are away from home?" Some quite vile stuff was being said and she added, "My husband is at home but he knows am safe we tha pickets." A voice from behind me shouted, "You'd be safe in a brothel." An even louder voice from within our ranks shouted, "Shut up!" I'll never forget one continuous chant that is tame in comparison but it went like this; 'Maggie Thatcher, Maggie Thatcher with her band of men (pointing to us) robs from the poor gives to the rich, robin bitch, robin bitch!'

There were times when I had one to one chats with some of the pickets and with some small groups too, whilst I joined them for a warming at their brazier. None of the other pickets seemed to object to their mates being friendly to me. They seemed to accept me a bit more because I had a Geordie accent. If we engaged in conversation, I told them about my background. I could talk pit language and about the life the miners had. I don't think I need to go over everything again because I said what needed to be said, at the beginning of my tale. Suffice it to say, you the reader will know of the admiration which I have for the coal miners. I'd be odd if that wasn't so, being that I am the first Curry to break with the pit tradition in occupation, including initially my two brothers.

It grieved me when I saw a headline in the paper. I cannot remember the exact figure now but it said for example, 'Pitmen earn £500 a week,' giving the impression they all did. Some might have, say a blaster at the coal face with danger money, on bonus and with overtime etc. but how many of them were there? It was pure sensationalism on behalf of the journalist to sell papers. The many ordinary and relatively unskilled men who worked down the pit did not get anything near what the papers said in wages. The large workforce, who worked on bank, (on the surface) was even more poorly paid.

One thing I did not do, was to let my friendliness go too far and for it to become fraternisation. Nor was I talking to them whilst acting as a spy. Neither did I put myself out to be with them. If I was close by and it happened, so be it. On no occasion did I spend more than a few minutes with them. I made it known, if it needed to be said, that first and foremost I was a copper. I was there in that role but that did not mean I could not see their argument too. I have always been conscious that a cop should remain impartial.

 I can give an example of what I believe to be fraternisation and a betrayal of impartiality, at a recent event. I was shocked to see the cops bending their knees at the 'Black Lives Matter' protest in London. My honest opinion is that they did it only to ingratiate themselves with the protesters and by doing so they betrayed the concept of a copper's impartiality. I believe disciplinary action should be taken against every one of them.

I was pleased to see the end of the Miners Strike and by that I mean, so I could get back to coppering and not that I was necessarily pleased with the end result. Back at Hastings, I attacked my job with the same enthusiasm that I had always had and retained right to the very end.

JEVINGTON AIR CRASH

At about 11 pm on Tuesday, 13 November 1984, I was off duty and about to go to bed when my telephone rang. It was the nick and I was called out to attend an air crash at Jevington near Eastbourne, East Sussex. A Rockwell Area Commander 690B light aircraft had crashed, killing all 9 occupants. The chartered flight had taken off from Dublin and was en route to Paris.

The first thing we had to do was to search the wide area for survivors, albeit that was unlikely. The search was carried out by forming a police line and combing the area by torchlight and by launching rocket flares to illuminate the vicinity. We crossed muddy ploughed fields, frequently sinking and becoming stuck in the mud, with the cold wind and rain lashing us.

I had over the years, spent time on duty out in dreadful weather. Many times, for example, I had directed traffic in bad conditions, when the sea breached the coastal defences, both at Worthing and Hastings. However, that winter's night at Jevington was off the scale for wildness. I was to spend the worst night of my police career, the largest part standing in an open ploughed field, without any shelter whatsoever.

I was sited near to the main part of the fuselage, which had to be guarded to protect the scene. It was later found that the aircraft had disintegrated at 19,000 feet and so wreckage was scattered over a wide area.

The weather throughout the whole of that winter's night was foul with driving rain and wind. I was soaked through, freezing cold and there was no let-up in the bad weather all night. I thought the morning daylight would never come. At one stage I sat down in the mud, just to avoid being blown over. There was no relief for any of us and no food or hot drinks. I reminded myself many times, that my temporary suffering was nothing compared to the fate of the 9 crash victims.

I also thought of my young Uncle, who was killed at the Battle of the Somme in WW1. How the field I stood in, must have had some, albeit slight resemblance to the battlefield, especially when the flares were set off. The big difference being, I was lucky because I was not in danger of losing my life and I knew my situation would very soon be over.

The morning did dawn and it was hard to tell if I was in police or army uniform, being that I was covered in mud. The police issue uniform was not fit for the hammering it took that night. Together with others, I had been in the open without respite for over 8 hours. We had been ill-prepared clothing-wise and unaware of the conditions of the night ahead. There was a great urgency for us to get out there to search and secure the wide area. All of us cops who were out in an open position that night were close to hypothermia and collapse.

I found out later, that the aircraft was en route to Paris to take part in the Beaujolais Nouveau Day festival when the new wine would be released at 12.01 am on the third Thursday of November. (2 days later.)

I have deliberately not gone into any detail of the casualties or to say exactly what I saw that sad and grim night because to do so would be to disrespect their memory and is entirely inappropriate.

How tragic I thought, that the 9 poor crash victims had lost their lives, choosing to fly at night in such atrocious weather conditions and only in pursuit of merely celebrating and being among the first to acquire a new batch of wine.

No cause for the accident was attributed, as there was not enough wreckage recovered to identify the cause. However, the Air Accident Investigation Branch report suggested a total electrical failure, which would have caused the autopilot to disengage, and the aircraft going into a terminal and unrecoverable spin.

EN ROUTE TO THE CONSERVATIVE CONFERENCE

In 1985, I was one of many sent to Bournemouth to police the Conservative Party Conference. I had met a dear cop called Roy Millar at Hastings and he and I immediately got on like house on fire. He was a broad Scot, me a Geordie and I said I was Roy's interpreter. Now I need to explain that Roy was a real fun guy but out of the two of us, it was me who was the wit. Normally, I'd do the funnies and Roy would encourage and laugh. What Roy had was charisma with a capital C and everybody wanted to be his friend and I was very happy to have become a close one. He was also on the Bournemouth trip. So we sat together on the coach and shared a room when we arrived.

Other coaches filled with cops from all over Sussex, were also on their way. Chichester is on the way to Bournemouth and it was decided by the bosses, that all the coaches would rendezvous at Chichester nick. There we would enjoy a tea break on a football field adjacent. I'm not exactly sure but there may have been about 200 PCs present.

After we had the tea, we were told to muster by some temporary buildings on a piece of waste ground. We were to wear our helmets and so that told us there would be a degree of formality. Indeed that was to be the case and we were told the superintendent in overall charge of the trip wished to address us all. So we were all lined up, helmets on and brought to attention and Roy was next to me. The superintendent arrived and gave the order for us to stand at ease. He then stood at the top of half a dozen steps, being part of the nearby building and so he was raised on a makeshift rostrum. He started his address and it went something like this;

'Gentlemen, we are all members of the Sussex Police Force. We are on our way to Bournemouth to assist in the policing of the Conservative Party Conference. We will be operating on another force's patch. I expect every one of you to conduct yourselves in a manner that will only enhance the force's already good reputation. Any man who misbehaves or drinks to excess will be on the first train in the morning back to Sussex. He will be before the chief constable on a discipline charge in the afternoon. I hope I have made myself perfectly clear. Are there any questions?"

I noticed Roy put his hand in the air. The superintendent said, "Yes, what is your question?" Roy said, "Wat time's the train?" Well, everyone burst out laughing and the superintendent obviously could not hope to still control the 200 hundred of us.

He must have decided the best course of action was to go with the flow and he laughed too. It was absolutely brilliant, a classic and one that will live with me forever.

BACK TO NORMAL POLICING

You may recall that when I started in the police, I said that I gained a great deal of satisfaction in detecting offences of criminal damage, which I believe to be a motiveless crime. Whilst not considered to be the most heinous of crimes, if it is of a nominal value, I nevertheless took a keen interest in seeking out those who were mindless enough to indulge themselves in such idle matters.

I am also an avid supporter of our armed forces and of those who have served our country. My Dad's brother Andrew died of wounds in WW1. My Dad served in WW2. Duncan Morton, who I greatly admired and featured at some length, was a decorated war hero of WW2 and lost a leg at Dunkirk.

So when criminal damage and property with armed forces connections, i.e. a war memorial to the fallen, came together and to my attention, I was determined to do what I could to identify and bring the culprits to justice irrespective of their age.

So it was in about 1985 and coming up to Remembrance Day that my normal patrol duty took me to Alexander Park. I was shocked

246

to find that the war memorial sited in the park had been desecrated. The damage had not been reported and I had not been delegated to investigate it. I simply came upon it and but for my interest, I could have ignored it and continued on my way.

The War Memorial in Alexander Park Hastings

The large circular structure with a pillar in the centre stands in the middle of an open area of the park. It is made of stone and painted pure white with matt emulsion paint. Brass plates are fixed around the perimeter, bearing the names of the fallen. These plates had been forced off and stolen in the past but they had been replaced at the cost to the ratepayers. Although I was not appointed as the investigating officer, in that case, it enraged me so much, that I did make my own enquiries but sadly the crime was never detected.

On this occasion, I found that the whole of the lower part of the structure had been vandalised, with what I first thought to be black paint. It turned out to be shoe polish, the type that is dispensed in liquid form via a sponge. It was a total mess and Hastings council, at some considerable cost, had to pull out all the stops to have it erased in time for the 11 November service.

I soon formed the opinion that the culprits were at least two young girls because of the wording of some of the graffiti, i.e. Katie loves David and Carol loves Peter. It was my calculated guess that it was the girls who had done the writing and not the boys, otherwise, it likely would have read David loves Katie and Peter loves Carol. It also seemed the writings would more likely be girls than boys because of the content. I vowed to do whatever I could to track down the perpetrators.

I believed in time, I could detect the crime and I was so confident I started to prepare for court. I had the memorial photographed and obtained a witness statement from the council, as to the cost of the repair. I cannot recall exactly how much that was but it was several hundred pounds. I put the photographs and statement in a file and all I wanted now was the offender's identities.

For the next few months any free working moment through the day and evenings, I was in that park. I asked every young person that I saw if they knew a Katie, Carol, David or Peter. Katie or Carol separately would have been of interest but connected as being friends, it would then have become very interesting.

Eventually, my efforts paid off and I found someone who did know the girls and crucially where they lived. The two girls were aged about 14 years old and they were known to be friends. They lived close by and were known to frequent the park. I interviewed them and they both admitted the offence. They appeared before a juvenile court and were dealt with but I do not recall the result, which did not matter much to me, my job was done.

Even though the offenders were two young girls, this case gave me as much personal satisfaction as any I ever dealt with, including those of a much more serious nature.

I GIFT A BURGLAR TO A PROBATIONER PC

In about late 1986, in the early hours, at about 2 am, I was out on patrol in a marked police car on my own and I was parked up in Queens Road. I heard the smashing of glass and I drove along the road in the direction to where the sound had come from. I arrived outside a clothing shop, to see a male about to step out of the broken display window. I took hold of him just as a young probationary constable arrived. PC Liam Brigginshaw was that officer. I thought that the arrest of the burglar would do Liam more good in the eyes of our senior officers than myself and would get him noticed. A burglar of any description is considered within all police circles as a nick worth having. I told Liam to arrest him and to be the officer in the case. Liam was delighted to oblige. I recalled how pleased I was to arrest my first burglar.

At the police station, the burglar denied the facts, even though he was seen by two cops and was wearing an overcoat he'd stolen from the shop with a price label still attached. However, he changed his mind at court and was given a custodial sentence.

Years later, I was to learn that Liam had become a superintendent and had been posted to Worthing. As the new divisional commander, he assembled the Worthing officers and knowing I had been stationed at Worthing, he related the story of my having 'gifted him a burglar,' when he was a young cop starting out. He said that he had always appreciated my unique and generous gesture.

Liam later transferred to the Essex police force and was promoted to the assistant chief constable. In 2007, he was very tragically diagnosed with cancer and died. He was 42 years old. Liam might well have gone on to even higher promotion had he lived, for he was an extremely bright and kindly soul.

AN EXTREMELY VIOLENT AND DANGEROUS MAN

On 8 January 1987, I was working a late shift, when the following crimes were reported;

15.55hrs. Theft of a video recorder at a shop by a male. He shook off a salesgirl who tried to stop him and walked off.

16.40hrs.The attempted theft of a radio from a shop by a male. The manager gave chase and the radio was dropped. The offender pulled a knife and escaped.

17.30 hours. The aggravated burglary of a house by a male. The offender forced his way into a house using a large piece of wood.

Damaged walls/door with a knife and also threatened a witness with the knife.

Very early on, I suggested the offender was a local man, by the name of, Leonard Arthur Michael Tedham. I told CID but they were adamant I was wrong and they were right, in that it was another man. What's more, they were out looking for their suspect. I spoke to my Inspector and he had every faith in me, that I was correct. He said, "Let them look for their guy and you carry on looking for yours" and that is what happened.

18.40 hrs. We caught up with Tedham and after battling with him, he was arrested. He was indeed in possession of a knife.

In addition to the above criminal offences all day long, we received call after call, of hit and run road traffic offences. Tedham was in possession of the offending car when arrested.

He later admitted the offences and was charged with the criminal offences and in addition 22 road traffic offences.

He appeared at Hastings Magistrates Court and was remanded in custody. However, he later applied for bail and a Judge granted it and he was released.

On 2 April 1987, I was crewed with my regular partner, PC John Clarke, when we received a call to go to a flat in Linley Drive. When we arrived, we were met by the daughter of the occupant, an elderly female called Rita Parminter. She told us she had not seen her mother for some time and feared for her welfare. There was no reply at the flat and the curtains were all closed. I managed

251

to open a bathroom window without damaging it and I peered in. I saw an elderly female and it later transpired it was the occupant. She was slumped by the washbasin in a sitting position. What turned out to be a cloth belt from her raincoat was wrapped around her neck in a loop and the other end was around one of the taps. I formed the opinion that she had been dead for some time. I immediately viewed the death with suspicion and decided not to enter the building, to forensically protect the scene. I requested via my radio the attendance of all of the following; CID, forensic scenes of crime officer, photography department and the police surgeon. PC Clarke and I waited outside.

A detective sergeant arrived and he also looked through the window. I told him I was not happy that it was a suicide and that it would be prudent to treat it as a suspicious death, until such time that we could prove otherwise. He was not pleased with my being vocal and ordered me to stay outside. Surprisingly, with PC Clarke he went inside to look around, especially for a suicide note. After looking around, he cancelled everyone I had requested, except the police surgeon. The DS decided it was a suicide. He had made his mind up and obviously he was not going to change it. The police surgeon arrived and he examined the body. The DS told him he believed it was suicide but I told the police surgeon I was not happy it was.

 Eventually and after much debate, the police surgeon agreed with the DS and left. However, he returned about 10 minutes later and said he'd changed his mind and now he agreed with me. Now the DS had to re-request those, he had cancelled. I said to PC Clarke,

"Everyone's going to know now who was right from the start and who was wrong." He said, "How's that?" I said, "Because both of you two's fingerprints are all over that flat now and me, who saw the body first, mine are not anywhere."

A murder enquiry was launched. The thorough forensic team search found a set of bloody fingerprints under the sink. Guess who's? Leonard Arthur Michael Tedham that's who! My guy, who was remanded in custody but another Judge LET HIM OUT ON BAIL TO MURDER! He strangled the poor woman and with the belt from her own raincoat hung her on the tap, obviously in a desperate attempt to make it look like a suicide.

The DS was taken off CID and put back into uniform. I honestly believe that if I had not been there that day, there is a great possibility that death would have been recorded as a suicide.

Only another mere PC with my no shrinking violet character, without a desire to be promoted and thus, have no fear of being non-compliant, would have stood up to the long-serving, Hastings established DS. It was enough to sow doubt in the mind of the police surgeon. Thank goodness that he changed his opinion. If he had not, the outcome would have been too bad to contemplate.

In 1988, Tedham was sentenced to life imprisonment.

My information is that Tedham was released on licence in July 2015. He died of cancer a few months later on Christmas Eve.

COMMENDATION FOR 50 ARRESTS

I continued on motor patrol duties with PC John Clarke as my regular partner.

On 11 February 1987, we jointly received a chief constables commendation and it read;

'PC's T W Curry (AC980) and J C Clarke (AC 409) both patrol Hastings are commended for their initiative and attention to duty, whilst engaged on uniform patrol during the period 20 September 1986 until 9 January 1987, resulting in the arrest of 50 persons for a wide variety of offences, including theft, burglary, misuse of drugs and traffic offences.'

This was not an unusually high amount of arrests for me to be involved in during such a short period. It was only that my inspector at the time decided to keep a record to highlight it. My self-motivated workload and enthusiasm were retained throughout the whole length of my service.

Shortly after this, PC Clarke took an office job and I continued on motor patrol for a while and then I undertook lengthy periods in plain clothes again i.e. back to my comfortable jeans and T-shirts. (No CID suits, for me.) I continued to have good success in the detection of crime, together with the 3 other team members.

CHAPTER 10

FURTHER INJURY FORCES EARLY RETIREMENT

Whilst at a nightclub fracas, my partner PC Brigginshaw and I were both assaulted by a mob. Whilst on the ground I was violently kicked in the neck and the back. I hung on to the offender and he was nicked. My injuries gradually got worse. The new superintendent at Hastings tried his hardest to help with my rehabilitation by allowing me to go solo in plain clothes. I was allowed to come and go as and when I could manage but finally I had to admit defeat, after a year off sick. I was retired on medical grounds on 1st December 1989. My final testimonial from the chief constable read; 'his conduct was exemplary.'

An experienced, dedicated cop, at the top of his game, lost the job he loved. The thug who brought about the demise received 100 hours of community service.

In about 1990, I stopped using the asthma inhaler and I do not suffer from asthma anymore. As a result of my injuries, with daily medication, I can lead a relatively healthy and contented life.

CHAPTER 11

JACK REECE QPM AND THE BRIGHTON BOMBING

A good friend of mine was the late retired Detective Chief Superintendent Jack Reece who lived in Hastings. I had been friends with his brother, retired Superintendent Peter Reece, since 1970, when he was my section inspector at Worthing. I never did work under Jack and our friendship developed through his brother and our mutual interest in sea fishing, which only really came about after I was forced to retire.

Jack was a great detective and headed the enquiry into the IRA attack on the Grand Hotel, Brighton, at that time housing the attendees of the Conservative Party Conference on 12th October 1984. It was to become known simply as the Brighton Bombing. On retiring, Jack only received a Queen's Police Medal. I believe he deserved the highest award, that of a knighthood because he headed the successful enquiry into the most infamous crime, not just in the past decade or even century but of all time. It culminated in the arrest, conviction and imprisonment of the perpetrator, Patrick Magee who was later released after 14 years, under the Good Friday agreement.

We celebrate every November the 5th, the capture of Guy Fawkes for his part in the conspiracy and planting of his explosives to blow up the Houses of Parliament in 1605. The big difference between that and the Brighton Bombing is that his bomb did not explode and therefore did not injure or kill anyone, whereas the latter did and very nearly claimed the life of the then Prime Minister Margaret Thatcher.

I wrote on the 9th August 1994 to Lady Thatcher, later becoming a Baroness, asking her to consider Jack for a belated knighthood. The reply was that he had received a QPM award and I quote; 'where service personnel are concerned, recommendations very much depend upon references from senior officers, in this case, it would have been from the chief constable.' It appears from that statement, that whilst the chief constable, at the time Roger Birch, received his knighthood, albeit not specifically for the Brighton Bombing enquiry, he did not support the same award for Jack. I have witnessed others, such as sportsmen and those in show business, receive knighthoods for considerably less than Jack's great contribution to the maintenance of law and order. I believe the real reason he did not get a knighthood was because of the still sensitive issue of the Irish connection.

Sadly both Jack and Peter are now deceased. Jack never knew I wrote to the PM but Peter did.

In the late 90s, I became more interested in sea fishing, something I had dabbled in. I became particularly interested in big-game fishing. I especially wanted to hook a marlin. Jack was also a fantastic sea fisherman and held 3 world records for, black marlin, hammerhead shark and a 6-gill shark, weighing in at a whopping 1069 pounds.

Jack with his record-breaking, 1069lbs 6-gill shark.

CHAPTER 12

KENYA

On the advice of Jack, I decided to go to Kenya in pursuit of the marlin. I went on to catch many marlin and sailfish, tagging and releasing all but the first one of each that I caught. My 1st was given away to locals and consumed. On arriving back in the UK, I saw marlin on sale for £18 per kg. I gave a fish away worth £1,200'ish in the UK but in Kenya, it was about £60 but I was still followed around like the Pied Piper! I no longer fish.

Tom with his first 133lbs. striped marlin 'tiddler.'

I was to go on to visit Kenya annually for the next 5 years staying for periods of up to 4 months during the UK winters. My interest in fishing brought me in contact with many of the beach boys and local fisherman. I bought a local wooden dhow and painted the sail with the word 'Hijack,' which got me even more well known, along the Mombasa coast. I gave it the name because all the locals said, 'Hi Tom' to me and 'Hi Jack,' to my ex-wife, Jackie. It was visible out at sea for miles and the only one with a name on the sail.

I gave the dhow to 3 young Kenyan's, the deal being that I would go to sea with them if they were not taking tourists out or fishing in earnest.

My dhow the 'Hi-Jack'.

Whilst I lived in luxury in a 5-star hotel, my heart ached for my fellow man and I did everything I could to try and improve the lives of some I came to be fond of. I paid by instalments for a stone house to be built for one of my newfound friends, Boris. He had previously lived in a thatched mud hut and supported his family, including his 90-year-old grandmother.

Many days these people survived on coconut and water only. How anyone can get to the age of 90+ under such bleak circumstances beats me but she did. On one occasion, I bought Boris a battery radio and one evening I visited him at his mud dwelling in the bush. The radio was playing at its loudest and his elderly grandmother was dancing. She only spoke Swahili and I said to Boris, "Tell her that we should take her to a discotheque." The dear lady answered by saying, "When?" The only personal possession she appeared to own, was the piece of cloth draped about her.

Whilst I was there, I ensured that the family had decent food every day and as I had given Boris a 1/3 share in the dhow, I hoped he'd get fish too. Unfortunately, it became apparent that whatever I did, it would eventually become undone. Boris, after the stone house was completed, gained some sort of status in the community and he married a woman with a child and she then became pregnant with his child. There were arguments about the dhow over the years and they only came to me when it needed money spent on it, for a new sail or such like. Boris went on to con a friend of mine from the UK out of thousands of pounds.

I witnessed the behaviour of tourists and in particular, fellow UK travellers, which was thoughtless. Such as the bartering for wood carvings and offering in exchange items, such as old trainers and T-shirts that obviously had been taken to Kenya for such a purpose but should have gone in the dustbin. Some were not fit to even give away. I gave mine away but they were always in decent condition. These guys wanted cash to put something in the cooking pot, not rubbish. I often saw a tourist barter a kid into the ground for an item and then seemingly walk off proud with their accomplishment, hand in hand along the beach with their spouse. They had no idea of what these poor people suffered every single day. I heard tourists say, "I've got ballpoint pens, they love them?" In the 21st century, no, they do not! They'll take them, as they do with anything because they are free but it is cash or food they want foremost.

Whilst suffering went on outside the guarded hotel, I saw tourists at the restaurant self-service pile their plates high with food only to leave half. It was then scraped into a bin and then emptied on an open space at the rearmost part of the hotel. There it would lie in the 40-degree sun, in a pile being picked over by monkeys, huge reptiles, rats and covered with plagues of flies. After days, the rotting pile would be shovelled onto a lorry and would be taken for disposal, at the Mombasa dump. When the lorry arrived at the dump, hundreds of people would excitedly chase after it, to be the first to get to the stinking mess.

The shock of this pathetic scene shamed and humbled me, for thinking I'd had a raw deal as a kid in Amble, by UK standards yes, by world standards absolutely not.

The whole country is corrupt from the top to the bottom. I regularly saw the police taking money from the locals at roadblocks. A short stay tourist only sees a roadblock and the police speaking to local motorists and could be forgiven for thinking they are looking for traffic offences. The majority of vehicles have bald tyres and holes in the floor in any case. What the police with their guns are doing, is taking 100 Kenya shillings (70p. but a waiter only earns 80ks. for a 12/14 hour shift) from every local motorist, under threat of arrest on a trumped-up charge. I got to see this because I travelled about in locals' cars.

The police don't stop a white tourist in a taxi and they do not because they are under strict orders not to, for fear of damaging the country's reputation and the crucial tourist trade. I witnessed them order a local to drive his open back truck to the police station and the thatching on the back was unloaded and stacked in the station yard, which looked like a farmyard. The driver did not have the 100 Kenyan shillings and so his thatching was kept until he returned with the money.

I witnessed a beach-boy friend being beaten by a policeman, who was demanding money. I stopped him and we had a fierce row. I went to the police station and I made a complaint. The officer in charge denied all knowledge of any such goings-on, even though it was widely known that he sent his officers out to do it and took his share of whatever was brought back. I told him if I did not have a letter from him after I returned to the UK as to the result of my complaint, I would write to the commissioner in Nairobi. He didn't write and I wrote to the commissioner and he did not reply. I wrote again and I said in the letter that his officer on the beach was corrupt, as was the officer I complained to and if he did not respond it must be because he too was corrupt. I told him if I did not get a reply, I would write to the president at the time, Moi. I did not get a reply and I wrote to President Moi. I got a reply saying and I quote; 'His Excellency commends you for your actions and has ordered a full investigation.' I still have the letter bearing the presidential seal. Months later I wrote again, asking what had happened and then again I wrote but there was no response. My last letter was to tell President Moi that he was as corrupt as his cop on the beach.

The following year, I returned to Kenya and my ex-wife was saying, "They'll be waiting for you!" and she believed it too.

Years later, Moi stood down as Kenya's president and he was investigated for mass corruption. Those who investigated him were Kenyans and nothing came of it.

On my next visit, I went to the divisional HQ to resurrect the complaint. I saw the Kenyan police district commissioner. He arrived in full uniform, seated in the rear of a chauffeur-driven black limousine, with a small flag flying at the front. He was greeted by salutes and I was ushered into his office. I reported the facts of my complaint to him and showed him the president's letter with the seal, which appeared to stun him. He of course also denied any knowledge of police corruption. I told him I was a retired UK, top cop. (top PC, I meant.) He got on the telephone and I heard him tell the officer at the local station, to immediately transfer the bullyboy cop to Nairobi, 300 miles away. He was never seen by the locals again. I was told that whilst I was in his area, if I experienced any further police problems whatsoever, to contact him directly.

By the time I left the DC's office, I knew him to be no intellectual. This was confirmed by a request he made. He said to me, "Sir, will you honour me by signing my book?" I expected it to be a visitor's book but from his drawer, he produced an autograph book which I signed thus, 'To my dear friend DC (his name) from Tom Curry. (Retired) Police Sussex, UK.' After I signed his book, I placed my hand on his heavily gold braided epaulette and with a big grin I said, "Do you think I am a movie star?" He said with an equal grin, "No sir, but you are a big police chief from England." I did not want to disappoint the old boy and so I just simply shook his hand

and left. However, I was to be as stunned, as the DC was when he saw the president's letter and seal, when it was insisted that I be escorted by a police car, with blue light flashing back to my hotel. It must have looked very odd indeed because my limousine was a local's car, without a flag, falling to bits, with cracked windscreen and smooth tyres.

I became aware that if a poor Kenyan dies, frequently a doctor does not see the deceased to certify the death. So there is no post mortem carried out, unless in a very rare case if the family arrange it and pay. In most cases, there is no birth certificate and therefore there is no record of even the existence of that person and on death, no record of that too. I'm not saying that in Kenya there is no compulsory post mortem requirement for suspicious deaths. However, in practice, it does not happen when it comes to the poor because no one in authority is aware and nor does it seem that anyone cares. In the majority of cases, the body is taken by the family and just buried, often irrespective of who owns the land. What occurred to me was how many deaths would be of natural causes and how many would be suspicious i.e. Murder. In the UK, murder detection rates soared when compulsory post mortems for suspicious cases of death, was adopted and enforced.

I thought of Boris' grandmother and the family's daily struggle for food. I wondered how many begrudged their elders the small amount of food they consumed. I also thought how easy it would be to hurry their end by any method available and to then dispose of the body without any outside interference whatsoever. On my visits to Mombasa I would think, how many murders will I pass today? Those who commit murder, in Kenya and the many other countries throughout the world that take death so casually, will remain at large until strict procedures are adhered to for all.

I will now describe an incident on the beach that puts it into the perspective of how little a Kenyan's life is worth in that country. One day two dolphins came up on the beach. One repeatedly beached itself and died, the other was encouraged to leave. Shortly after the beaching, a Kenya ministry of agriculture and fisheries van arrived with a flashing light. They obviously had heard 'on the jungle drums' of the dead dolphin and had come to collect it for dissection to discover the cause of its death. However, by the time the van arrived, there was no dolphin. It had already been dissected right there on the beach, for another purpose, that being for human consumption. The smell of cooking dolphin was already wafting across the beach, from fires instantly made by the beach boys and other pieces were at that precise time being transported home.

My point, which will be apparent by now, is a dolphin in Kenya appears to be worth more than human life and that can never be acceptable.

I could no longer continue seeing my fellow man suffer in that beautiful country and after 2000, I vowed never to return and neither will I ever visit another developing nation. What Kenya did teach me, was that if you are born in the UK life will always be better than it is in many countries, even if you are on the lowest level of income. Therefore we should be justly proud of our country and of our police service.

266

CHAPTER 13

CONCLUSION

After nearly 60 years in Sussex, although my broad Geordie accent has somewhat softened, it appears I can still write in it when quoting those who never lost it. I have to say that in my adult life, I have never believed that my accent at any time was a bad thing. I have always felt accepted wherever I was and indeed I am sure it helped in my being remembered. I think it is true that you are not normally conscious of how you sound when speaking. I am not aware daily that my accent is still very noticeable. I am often surprised when a southerner says, "Where are you from?" Hoping to lead them into a trap, I always reply, "Northumberland" and if the desired "Which part?" is the response, I reply, "All of me," followed by, "How dare you? I've been in Sussex for over 50 years."

On the other hand, if I am back in Amble, I have been met with, "Wat are ee tarkin al posh fur? A na ee, you weren't broot up wi a silver spoon in ya gob." It appears that my accent is so intermingled it makes me an alien wherever I am. It is so jumbled maybe that is why I don't even know what I'm talking about half the time but that could also be my age! As for how it has remained as it has, when only the first 20% of my life was spent in the NE, I just do not know. The only explanation I can come up with is that maybe I am so absorbed in just what I'm saying, I have never listened to anyone else!

In 2007 my wife and I divorced, this time it was not my fault. I am now happily single again. Only my brother Ray and I are alive now from our family.

When I was first posted to Worthing in about February 1969, men who had been in the forces during WW2 were still serving. Many of those men were my mentors and role models. Much of what they taught me stayed with me throughout my service. I had no desire to change what I considered an efficient and productive way of policing. I never really put much effort into hounding the poor motorist. Most of the time, I dealt with such offences with a verbal caution rather than a booking.

My mentors having lived through a war understandably did not get too excited about a motorist doing 35 mph in a 30 zone. Neither could I, not when there were proper villains to be 'collared.'

It was a sad day around 1970, when those who had joined after the war, all completed their 30 years of service. (Most had 5 years of military war service, to count towards their pension.) They retired almost overnight and en masse and we lost the backbone of policing. A new breed of cop was to be born, one with educational degrees. In my book, any such degree should not take precedence over good old fashioned common sense. Being a good operational cop does not require a degree but the latter is a must.

Right from day one, promotion, promotion was rammed home. I never took the promotion exam and so I was never considered for promotion. I was never interested because they gave me a whistle, truncheon and pocketbook but in the ensuing melee, they must have forgotten to issue me with ambition. For a kid with little hope, in a dying pit village, to cop was a big leap for me and just being a PC, did 'Wor Tomis The Polis,' just fine.

CID never appealed really because I liked being on the streets and from nothing, I was frequently able to spot something that was not quite right and with equal ease sniff out a wrong 'un. That was what gave me the biggest thrill and I enjoyed the excitement of the chase and the ultimate capture.

Many times, I was asked by a senior officer what my hobbies were. I always found that question particularly difficult because in truth, the police was not only my job but I viewed it also as my hobby. I lived and breathed the police. I never did tell anyone that because I feared it would not be believed and would be thought to be a reply from someone wishing to mislead or impress.

I occupy some of my time now, assisting friends or friends of a friend, free gratis, with maybe a consumer problem or such like. Many I support via the small claims court. It keeps my brain active and my sense of justice is still as strong as it ever was. I've always championed the underdog because I've been there!

Since I retired I have made many citizen arrests, even though I have chronic back pain and I'm getting older by the minute. On one occasion a retired cop on the enquiry desk at Hasting nick said to my mate Roy Millar, "Why does he get involved?" Roy simply said, "Because he does and what's more he's made more arrests since he retired than you ever did in the 30 years when you were in the job!" I must be slipping as my last involvement was 6 years ago. I really must try and get out and about a bit more.

In 2014, at the age of 65 years, I witnessed a group of youths fighting in Hastings Town Centre. One of them produced a 13" carving knife and ran amok chasing the others. Although it was daylight and very busy, no one made a move except me. He dumped the knife in a waste bin, which I recovered. I saw him remove his coat and run off. Ahh! I thought, our boy's been nicked before and is conscious of being identified on description. A slight change in his dress might fool an amateur and less competent witness.

About 20 minutes later, a long way from the scene and in company with a uniform cop, I identified him. He said looking at my shorts and perhaps my grey hair, "Who are you? You ain't a cop." I said, "No, I'm not but I'm still the guy who's going to get you locked up!" I was the only witness no one else came forward.

The next day, he only got a 26 weeks custodial sentence. I received no thanks from anyone, including the police but that will not deter me. Why don't I just mind my own business? It's simple, I was once a cop and it looks like I'm always going to think like a cop! (Retired).....and maybe I just like to keep my hand in!

I've enjoyed reliving my memories through the writing of this book and I hope it makes for an enjoyable read too.

STAY SAFE.

WOR TOMIS THE POLIS